From reviews of *The Imperfect Homeschooler's Guide to Homeschooling* (eBook version):

"What a find! It's been a while since I read something on homeschooling that really fired me up. I loved this book and its fresh take on homeschooling and the commitment it requires. No homeschooling parent does it perfectly. Together though, we can learn from one another and do our best for our children. That's what Barb is striving to do by sharing what she has learned along the way. It is a blessing!

....I have thoroughly enjoyed this book and would highly recommend it! The only thing that could make it better is offering it in a printed version, but that's my personal preference. This book inspired me and gave me a ton of great ideas and tips. It's nice to know I'm not the only one out here that falls under the "Imperfect Homeschooler" banner!"

Lisa Barthuly,
The Old Schoolhouse Magazine

See full review at
http://www.thehomeschoolmagazine.com/Homeschool_Reviews/2039.php

"This is a MUST read! This book is perfect for those just beginning to think about homeschooling, or those who have been at it a while . . . It has new ideas in it, unlike many homeschool books that just repeat information that can be found in a dozen other homeschool books."

Tara B.
Homeschooling parent

D0028357

"Reading *The Imperfect Homeschooler's Guide to Homeschooling* is like having another mom who is farther along on the road look back to see you struggling, turn around to come alongside, put an arm around your shoulders, and lighten your load with encouragement and advice.

....The advice in this book rings true, and it is clear to me that this author has drawn from experience and not merely theory in writing this guide. Altogether *The Imperfect Homeschooler's Guide to Homeschooling* is a guide that any homeschooler, newcomer or veteran, should find helpful and encouraging."

Jean Hall
Eclectic Homeschool Online

See full review at:
http://eclectichomeschool.org/reviews/individual_review2.as
p?revid=2089

"I've been homeschooling for the last 10 years, and still have those moments when I want to throw in the towel. Your book helped me remember the reasons we are homeschooling. We have 8 children and this year we will have 6 in school. Thank you!"

Kathy Gettig
Homeschooling parent

THE IMPERFECT HOMESCHOOLER'S

GUIDE TO HOMESCHOOLING

A 20-Year Homeschool Veteran Reveals How to Teach Your Kids, Run Your Home and Overcome the Inevitable Challenges of the Homeschooling Life

Barbara Frank

Cardamom Publishers
Sturgeon Bay, Wisconsin

The Imperfect Homeschooler's Guide to Homeschooling
Copyright © 2008 Barbara Frank
All rights reserved

Published by
Cardamom Publishers
P.O. Box 4
Sturgeon Bay, WI 54235

Printed in the United States of America

ISBN 978-0-9742181-2-0

Library of Congress Control Number: 2008901494
Library of Congress Subject Heading: Home schooling

To the many dedicated women I've known who homeschooled their children to adulthood, particularly Janet Amelio, Ann Galliers and Ann Muenster. I'm blessed to know you!

and

To my better half, my wonderful husband Tim:
"We are still maladjusted misfits, and we have loved every minute of it."

TABLE OF CONTENTS

ABOUT THIS BOOK

This book is an expanded edition of *The Imperfect Homeschooler's Guide to Homeschooling* eBook. It is more than twice the size of the eBook, and contains everything that was in the eBook, plus material originally published in "The Imperfect Homeschooler" newsletter or on "The Imperfect Homeschooler" Web site, at:

www.cardamompublishers.com/imperfect-homeschooler.htm

On that page, you will find a form for subscribing to "The Imperfect Homeschooler" newsletter, a free monthly e-mail newsletter of homeschool encouragement.

ABOUT THE AUTHOR

Barbara Frank is the mother of four homeschooled-from-birth children, ages 15–24, and a freelance writer and editor. She has a journalism degree from the University of Illinois.

Barbara is also the author of *Life Prep for Homeschooled Teenagers*, *Homeschooling Your Teenagers*, and the upcoming *Thriving in the 21st Century*. She blogs about homeschooling, parenting and related issues at:

http://barbaramfrank.blogspot.com

Feel free to contact her there with your homeschooling questions!

PREFACE

Homeschooling has been a big part of my life since the early 1980's. As soon as I read about the concept, it grew from a tiny seed ("Maybe we'll do this someday") to a decision ("I can't believe the school bus just left and I didn't put her on it") to a lifestyle. This is what our family does. We homeschool our children, and it has been a great blessing for our family.

Looking back, I can see where God used a variety of people, books and events to keep us on the homeschooling path until we reached the point where homeschooling became a given. Veteran homeschooling moms shared their experiences and beliefs with me, taking time out of their busy schedules to answer my sometimes panicked questions. Books like *Home Grown Kids* and *Dumbing Us Down* gave me hope that not only *could* we homeschool, but that it would be the best thing for our children's development. Witnessing our children's successes was the fuel that kept us going.

Since our oldest two children finished "high school homeschool" (we're still homeschooling two younger children), I have worked to encourage newer homeschooling parents through my writing projects and speaking engagements. It's my way of trying to give back a little of what I was given.

I began by writing *Life Prep for Homeschooled Teenagers*, a course I designed for my children when they were teens. Soon after its publication, my husband and I started "The Imperfect Homeschooler" Web site in order to encourage homeschoolers on this strenuous yet rewarding path they've chosen. The positive response I got from other homeschoolers led me to expand my work by publishing three booklets about homeschooling. This book includes the contents of those booklets, as well as articles from my monthly newsletter, "The Imperfect Homeschooler."

Whenever I write about homeschooling, I have a goal of encouragement. I hope that by sharing with readers the information and insight I've gleaned over two decades of homeschooling my own children, I can make it a little easier for them to stay the course. People who give up on homeschooling, despite their best intentions, often do so because they become discouraged. When one of my books or articles helps someone work through and past that feeling of discouragement to the rewards that await their family, then I've done my job.

I hope that this book encourages you by guiding you through the inevitable decisions and rough patches that everyone encounters on the homeschooling path. Should you have questions that are not answered in this book, feel free to e-mail me at cardamompublishers@sbcglobal.net, and I'll try to help in any way I can.

Best wishes on your homeschooling journey,

Barbara Frank
December 2007

CONFESSIONS OF AN IMPERFECT HOMESCHOOLER

In this section, I'll explain why I call myself "The Imperfect Homeschooler," share a bit of background on my family, and offer some basic homeschooling advice before we get into specifics in upcoming sections.

Why the *Imperfect* Homeschooler?

Welcome to *The Imperfect Homeschooler's Guide to Homeschooling*! Before we get into a discussion of homeschooling, let me tell you a bit about myself.

I've been homeschooling my four children for the past 20 years. I just want to share a few details about each of them:

Sarah (24) is the CEO of a Fortune 500 company she started when she was 16. She lives in a lakefront home she designed herself. Her goal is to replace Oprah Winfrey as America's Richest Woman.

Peter (23) won the National Spelling Bee and the National Geography Bee the year he turned 12. After scoring a 37 on the ACT, he started college at 14, but just graduated this year; he had to put his college career on hold for a few years while NASA tapped him to lead their Mars research team.

Mary (17) plays seven instruments (you can hear her playing the harp at homeschool conventions nationwide) and speaks four languages fluently. She began reading at the age of six months, thanks to the phonics tapes I played through headphones on my belly during my pregnancy with her.

Joshua (15) isn't really college material, but he did start his own software company last year. Movers and shakers in tech circles believe he will be the successor to Bill Gates.

Despite my children's accomplishments, I must admit that they're really just normal kids. They do *all* the housework, cooking and home repairs. In fact, right now my sons are replacing the roof! My husband and I couldn't be prouder, and feel that our children are living proof of the success of homeschooling!

We live on a picturesque 500-acre farm in the Midwest, where we raise our own organic fruits, vegetables and livestock. (Needless to say, we were fully prepared for Y2K.) In our spare time, we practice singing (our family choir CD just won a Grammy award) and reciting the names of the U.S. Presidents in order.

Are you impressed? Don't be; only the first two paragraphs are true. I *do* have four children ages 15–24, and they *have* been homeschooled from birth. But that's where any similarity between them and the children I described above ends.

Let's face it, as the success of the homeschooling movement has become more visible, stories about homeschooling families and their accomplishments have become commonplace. Many of the families featured can make us feel downright inferior, especially those described in some homeschooling magazines. My web site and newsletter are called "The Imperfect Homeschooler" because I want to reassure readers that *they don't have to be perfect parents in order to homeschool.*

You see, when I first began researching homeschooling, it appeared to me that homeschooling parents must be unusually gifted in raising children. I developed that misconception after regularly reading a major homeschool magazine. At the time, it was my lifeline; one of only two places (the other was a wonderful little newsletter put out by Raymond and Dorothy Moore) where I could learn about homeschooling, a revolutionary idea back then.

Every issue of that homeschooling magazine had a cover shot of a real, live homeschooling family. It was usually a large family, with Mom holding a newborn and Dad holding a toddler, and four or six other children all about 18 months apart each. And all the kids would not only be dressed alike, but would actually be looking in the same direction at the same time! And Mom and Dad would have these calm expressions that said, "We know what we're doing."

And because I'm a masochist, I'd flip to the cover story and read about this family and how all their children had memorized large chunks of the Bible, and were accomplished musicians, geography bee winners, scored in the 99th percentile on standardized testing, and never gave their parents any trouble because their parents were raising them to be obedient to God and to them.

This made me feel so inadequate. Yet I kept reading these cover stories as soon as each issue arrived. And the message that I got from them was, if we do it *just right*, if we follow the Biblical advice on child-rearing and homeschool our children, they'll turn out like the kids on the cover of the homeschooling magazine: Perfect Children.

Well, maybe those parents had it all figured out, but even though I only had two small children at that time, I could already see that "perfect children" and "perfect parents" are oxymorons, like "jumbo shrimp" or "definite possibility." We are all sinful, and there has only ever been one Perfect Person on earth, who started out as the Perfect Child. The rest of us are, well, imperfect.

And that's my point. We are not capable of being perfect homeschoolers; we must accept our imperfections. I don't want anyone who reads my work or visits my site to get the idea that they must be perfect homeschooling parents in order to successfully homeschool their children. I don't pretend to be perfect, and I make it clear that my children are not perfect, either. Yet despite our imperfections, homeschooling has been a wonderful blessing for our entire family.

Recently I flipped through some back issues of that homeschooling magazine. I came away from the task rather depressed, and then I remembered once more why I stopped subscribing to that magazine.

I'm sure the publisher did not intend to make readers feel bad about themselves and their homeschooling efforts. But if the tone of that magazine depressed someone like me, who has already successfully homeschooled two children from birth through high school, what might it do to someone who has just begun? Or to someone who is struggling just now, and hasn't homeschooled long enough to find out that we all struggle at times? I worry that people like that will give up, and miss out on so many wonderful homeschooling experiences because they feel like they'll never produce perfect children.

But homeschooling parents who write articles about their lives don't have perfect children, either. They just want to use their children's successes to encourage others with examples of what homeschooling can produce.

When an article in a homeschooling magazine makes *you* feel inadequate, consider that while the author is thrilled to inform you that her son Fritz scored a perfect 1600 on the SAT, she'd never write an article describing how he wasn't potty-trained until he was six. There's always the rest of the story that you don't know, because no one is perfect.

So if you agree that no one is perfect, and that no one is capable of homeschooling perfectly, then you'll understand why I like the phrase "The Imperfect Homeschooler." **We are all imperfect homeschoolers**. In this book, I hope to encourage you instead of making you feel inadequate. Just by making the choice to homeschool your children, you have put them on the right track.

What I Know About Homeschooling

One of my pet peeves is homeschool speakers or writers who have no homeschooling experience. Years ago, I actually attended a homeschooling seminar where I discovered that the speaker on the topic "How to Teach Your Children" *had* no children! Naturally, her advice held no weight with me.

I want to hear from people who have lived what they are teaching, and I'm sure you do, too. I want you to know that this book is the result of experience, not untested theories. Thus, our homeschool testimony:

My husband Tim and I are the parents of four children, all homeschooled from birth:

Sarah (24): homeschooled through high school, lives on her own in a small Midwestern city where she is assistant manager for a retail/online business.

Peter (23): homeschooled through high school, 2007 college graduate and newlywed, manager in a publishing company, hopes to eventually attend seminary.

Mary (17): currently homeschooling high school, plays violin, loves to sew and create Web sites and graphics.

Joshua (15): homeschooled, has Down syndrome, loves drawing, writing, video games and hanging out with friends.

Our Homeschool Beginnings

I first learned about homeschooling by reading the works of Dr. Raymond and Dorothy Moore (their books are great!) I began homeschooling my older children using "The Weaver," a unit studies curriculum I highly recommend. That worked fine the first year. But I thought first grade was supposed to be more challenging, so I switched to traditional curriculum such as Bob Jones for Bible and A Beka for other subjects. That was a big mistake; we burned out within a few years.

From that experience, I learned to loosen up, to ditch what doesn't work and that you don't *have* to finish a textbook or workbook. I also discovered that when your homeschool is too structured, it's very easy to fall behind on your self-imposed schedule. To make matters worse, the kids get bored because they have no interest in what's being forced on them. If I wanted them to be bored, I could have sent them to school; *I* was always bored there!

It was time to try something different, so we began brainstorming. I asked the kids what they wanted to learn, and made a list of their responses. It was a long list! I used that list to find books and materials they would enjoy. Every so often, we'd have another brainstorming session, since their interests were always changing.

I knew my kids were much happier with this method, and was able to measure the results, thanks to achievement testing when they were 7 and 8. That gave me confidence, because it showed they were way ahead of grade level!

Another good way to relax your homeschool is to have more babies. I spent much of pregnancy #3 not feeling well, so I learned to adapt my teaching methods to being horizontal. I read aloud to the children even more than usual (they loved it!) and we relied less on formal written work.

Pregnancy #4 brought medical problems for me and the baby; he was born with multiple birth defects, including Down syndrome. He spent a month in the Neonatal Intensive Care Unit at a hospital nearly an hour away, then came home on a heart and breathing monitor. This resulted in several months of no school for the kids; instead, they played with building toys, colored, made crafts and read books. Since spring achievement testing had already been paid for, I took them . . . and found they'd each gone up two grade levels in one year, despite all the months of no school. Hmmmm . . .

Fast-forward to their teen years. Sarah, who wanted no part of college, scored a 24 on the ACT, which she took while suffering from the flu. Peter scored a 29 on the ACT (30's on all subjects but science, which was 25) and 1340 on the SAT. He received several scholarship offers, and was accepted to all six colleges to which he applied. Moral of this story: relax!

Some Important Lessons I've Learned about Curriculum

I've discovered that packaged curriculums don't work for us. That doesn't mean they won't work for anyone else, of course! Each family is unique.

I buy specifically for each child. I've learned not to assume one child will thrive on the materials a previous one loved, because each child is different. This is why I have a crawlspace full of books and educational games. Over time I developed a good eye for what works for whom; you will, too.

Don't worry about how you'll teach the hard stuff some-day, like Algebra 2. You'll be relearning everything as you go along and you'll not only understand it, you might enjoy it; I did!

Don't be afraid to let a younger child pass up an older sib-ling in an area he or she is good at. Let each child progress at his own pace. God has gifted each one differently.

Pray, pray, pray before setting foot in the exhibit hall of a homeschool convention. Otherwise, you'll be overwhelmed. Often, I spend the whole day perusing everything (taking notes, of course) and picking up every catalog I can find. Then I order things from home at my leisure, waiting until I have peace about what to buy.

Favorite Curriculum Sources

Rainbow Resource Center! (www.rainbowresource.com) The commentary in their catalog is extremely valuable, and their service is top-notch.

The Book Peddler (http://www.bookpeddler.us)

Timberdoodle Co. (http://www.timberdoodle.com)

Rod and Staff Publishers (especially their Bible curriculum and their preschool workbook series)

Usborne Publishing (http://www.usborne.com)

T.J.Maxx and Marshall's (educational toys, games and books at reduced prices)

Homeschooling Methods

Parents may follow certain methods (traditional, unschooling, etc.) but ultimately, each family develops its own, and it changes with time and each individual child. You'll learn to be flexible (which is exactly what government schools cannot do).

Remember:

• God chose your children specifically for you: who better to teach them?

• Pray for wisdom, grace, patience, and energy, because you can't do this alone.

• Don't make it harder than it needs to be.

• Limit running from homeschool group activity to park district class to Awanas, etc. Establish a home of peace.

• Enjoy your kids; homeschooling is a privilege and a blessing.

• Don't compare yourselves to others, *ever*! Keep praying for guidance if you feel like you're off course.

When You Shouldn't Homeschool

Don't do it if you and your spouse are not in agreement on this issue. If Dad's all for it but Mom needs to be coaxed, she's not going to put her heart into it. And if Mom wants to but Dad disagrees, she will get little or no support from him. My family could not have homeschooled all these years without the verbal and physical support of my husband (he vacuums and does dishes!) It's also important that you present a united front to any disapproving friends and relatives.

Expectations

Don't expect perfect days or perfect children. True, the Bible says "Train up a child in the way he should go, and when he is old, he will not depart from it." But that is a principle, not a promise. (If it were a promise, we could not have free will, and we have been given free will.)

Just do your best, pray unceasingly, and enjoy this time with your children. So many parents these days hardly see their children because someone else is raising them all day. You are blessed!

HOMESCHOOLING 101

This section gets into the nitty-gritty of homeschooling: how, when and where you do it. You'll also find a list of helpful tools and books you'll appreciate, and advice for getting the most from homeschool conventions. Please don't look at this section as carved-in-stone rules; I'm just sharing what worked for us.

Where's the Schoolroom?

When people find out I teach my children at home, it seems they always want to know if we have a schoolroom. Maybe they think having a schoolroom is necessary for learning, or perhaps they picture their own school years spent in a room with rows of desks and a utilitarian clock on the front wall. They often assume I've recreated that room somewhere in our house.

In reality, homeschooling has taken place in almost every part of our house. We began at our kitchen table when my daughter was five and my son was four. We'd work at the kitchen table until lunchtime, then put our books and supplies away in a plastic box and set the table for lunch. For a few years, it really was that simple.

Then we had more children. During my pregnancies, I would often be so nauseated or exhausted that it was all I could do to make it to the sofa, so that's where we had school. By the time child #3 arrived, the kitchen table wasn't working for us anymore. The kids tired of cleaning up their homeschooling messes in order to eat lunch. Sometimes they had a project they couldn't move, or a craft that had to lay flat until it dried. So we graduated to a table set up in our rarely-used living room. Once Baby became mobile, we put a playpen next to the table so she could play contentedly while we worked.

Her content did not last long. We moved to the dining room table, and put up a gate to keep her away from tempting

11

items like markers and glue sticks. By now, the big kids were working at a level where they needed to concentrate, so it was better to keep their little sister away from their work area. At this point, we had also accumulated quite a few books, so we bought a wall's worth of bookshelves and put them in the dining room, too.

Child # 4 arrived, along with an apnea monitor to which he would remain tethered every day for over a year. This required a lot of my attention (it seemed like his heart rate would slow down and set off the alarms whenever I was in the middle of explaining an algebra problem), so the big kids often did their work alone in the dining room. Being kids, at some point they would begin annoying each other. This eventually got bad enough that Dad brought home an enormous piece of cardboard, which we used as a divider so our children couldn't distract each other because they couldn't see each other. I tried to ignore the wads of paper that were sometimes shot over the barrier. (I can laugh at this now.)

As the younger two got older and noisier, the big kids began asking to do their schoolwork in their bedrooms. This seemed like a good idea, and sometimes it even worked out. But most of the time, they'd become distracted by their possessions and would not get their work done. So I usually made them work in the dining room, while I restricted the younger two to the family room, where I plied them with special toys (reserved for school time) and Barney videotapes.

Back at the kitchen table, I began working with #3 on her preschool workbooks. (She had requested her own school work because she wanted to be like the big kids.) As for #4, much of his time was spent on the family room floor, where we practiced his physical therapy. On the days he had therapy appointments, our school was held in the therapy center's waiting room. All three older kids worked on their schoolwork there, while I watched our little guy and his therapist.

Eventually, we had big kids reading in their bedrooms, doing math in the dining room, making craft projects in the basement and learning to cook in the kitchen. We had little people playing with clay on the patio, reading with me on a blanket under a backyard tree, and listening to math-fact tapes in the car. For our little guy, bath time was often spent teaching him how to pour water from cup to cup or practicing his speech sounds.

For many years, almost every room in our house was a schoolroom, proving that learning is not restricted to a single room with a row of desks and a clock on the front wall. Kids learn everywhere, and that's why homeschooling occurs all over the house. It also occurs beyond the house: in the car en route to activities or on vacation when we visit historic sites or museums. Far beyond our neck of the woods, there are families who homeschool on farms and ranches, or while traveling in foreign countries, or even in boats as they sail around the world. Ultimately, the question should not be "Where's the schoolroom?" but "Who needs a schoolroom?"

How Many Hours?

One of my least favorite questions from people who don't homeschool is, "How many hours a day do you homeschool?"

Let's face it, answering this question is like tip-toeing through a minefield. Depending on the viewpoint of the questioner, you may not be doing enough, or you may be overdoing it. The former is usually the case, but in either case, your answer may not be what they want to hear.

I'm often asked that question by new or prospective homeschoolers, too. Faced with the proposition of recreating the seven or eight-hour day they remember from their own school years, they wonder how they're going to be able to fill those hours, and whether they can handle it.

I like to tell them the story of my stint as a Sunday school teacher at my church. I began teaching Sunday school after I had been homeschooling for about ten years. Needless to say, I was accustomed to working one-on-one with my kids, which is a pretty efficient way to teach, and to learn. Of course, I knew that I couldn't expect the same efficiency when teaching 10 or 12 fourth-graders for an hour, but I still didn't realize the extent to which it would be different.

Every Saturday night, I diligently read the teacher's guide and the Bible lesson, and made a list of activities as suggested by the lesson plan. Since those were usually rather dry, I'd throw in a few ideas of my own, including a game, or a passage from a book . . . something to make things more interesting. To me, it was important that we had enough activities to do. I didn't want to find myself standing in front of the class with 15 minutes to go and nothing left to do with them.

I needn't have worried. I soon discovered that it was going to be impossible to even start class on time. Kids trickled in for about the first ten minutes, and each one's arrival interrupted what we were doing. Taking attendance was not as easy as it sounds, because the kids would interrupt each other with stories of what they'd been doing lately, or they'd ask me for a drink of water or permission to visit the restroom.

Once we got started on the lesson, we'd be interrupted by dropped or broken pencils, someone kicking someone else under the table, someone falling out of their chair (this happened fairly often), or someone who had a question because they hadn't been listening.

I still recall the day I was trying to get through to them the concept of Jesus' resurrection. They seemed interested, and they were asking good questions, but then one young man raised his hand, and when I called on him he very seriously informed the class and me that his dog liked to eat breath mints. The rest of the class burst into laughter, he looked around confused at their reaction, and I realized any impact my lesson had made was now lost.

I taught Sunday school for five years, and I hope my students learned what they needed to know. What I learned is that teaching in a classroom setting can be very inefficient, especially when compared to homeschooling. I was accustomed to accomplishing a lot in a little time with my kids, but when it came to Sunday school classes, I learned that it was a good day if I accomplished anything.

Sunday school class lasts an hour. Multiply that by seven or eight to get an idea of how much inefficiency you'd find over the course of a day of formal school. Getting everyone into their seats, taking attendance, quieting them down...and that may be for each class period. Then there's the misbehavior, the back-talk ...all those things that kids do when they're determined to keep the teacher off-track.

Let's compare that to homeschooling. By giving our children our undivided attention for a while, we can answer their questions, share information with them, and make sure they understand what we've taught them. It's pretty simple and straightforward, and it doesn't take several hours a day. I usually tell new homeschoolers that in the early years, I spent maybe an hour (90 minutes tops) "doing school" with my kids. By high school, it was more like an hour or two working with them, and an additional hour or two of them working independently.

Most non-homeschoolers don't need that much information, though. They are really asking me if my children are getting what they need to become "educated," as society sees it. If I give them an actual number of hours, they may not approve because we've only ever done a few hours a day of formal study. A quoted number of hours wouldn't be accurate anyway, because like most homeschooled kids, mine have learned many more things outside of formal study than they have from it.

What I've found works best when non-homeschoolers ask how many hours of school we do each day is replying, "As many hours as it takes." It seems to satisfy them, and I know it's an honest answer, because my children are learning throughout their waking hours. It also forces *them* to put a number to it; since they're accustomed to the inefficient ways of public schools, they're probably thinking of a larger number of hours than I am. Works for me!

What I Did On My Summer Vacation......School?

When summer arrives, it's time to put away the books and dig out the suntan lotion and the beach toys, right? Well, for some people, it is. But for many homeschoolers, summer vacation doesn't really exist.

When I first began homeschooling, we took the summers off. The neighbor children were on vacation from public school, and my children wanted to play outside with them. That worked well for a few years, but as the neighbor kids got older, they started sleeping in until noon, so my children didn't have anyone to play with until after lunch. I got to thinking that we could have done a bit of study in the mornings without cramping their play time. I also came to realize that taking the summer off of school meant we often ended up doing an awful lot of review in September. Doing school during the summer didn't seem like a bad idea.

When you think about summer vacation, you realize that it's not an immutable law of nature. It's simply a habit we developed from all those years we went to school. Back then, having the summer off was one of our rights, a reward for spending the previous nine months locked up in school—we would have staged a revolt if summer vacation had been taken away from us.

But the truth is that it's just a tradition, and each of us needs to think about whether it works for our homeschooling family. My experience has been that some years taking a summer vacation worked for us, and other years, it didn't. We try different yearly schedules based on our needs. It is so nice once you realize you have that freedom!

For example, when spring came one year I realized just how far behind I was on housecleaning. I decided to take the summer off and tackle all the dusty nooks and crannies of my house (you'll find the details of that cleaning plan in the "On the Home Front" section of this book). When fall arrived, my house was much cleaner and we were rested and ready to start our schooling again.

But that was just one year. There were other years when we did school all summer. The kids slept in, spent the hot and humid mid-days inside, doing school in air-conditioning, and went to the pool or ran in the sprinkler in the late afternoons. Come September, we needed no review, and even took some time to go on vacation, visiting areas in Wisconsin that had been crammed with tourists during the summer, but were now quiet, with bargain hotel rates to boot. September weather is always nice there; we returned home relaxed and happy.

Another year, we took off three weeks during May. We drove to Florida to see the shuttle launch at Cape Canaveral, then visited other areas of that beautiful state. There were no crowds because the spring-break revelers had long-since gone back home, as had the snowbirds. There was very little traffic, and we found great off-season rates wherever we went. It was a wonderful vacation.

We continue to keep a flexible yearly schedule, trying to go with whatever works for us at that particular point in time. For several years, we did school four days a week year-round, with a week off here and there and two at Christmas. I used our weekly Friday off as a catch-up day; since the homeschool group we belonged to scheduled its field trips on Fridays, we had an occasional five-day school week. On our weeks off, we took off-season vacations, finding them to be low-stress and low-cost. How long did we keep that schedule? As long as it worked, which was up until a few years ago. Now that we have a high schooler again, we've gone back to five-day weeks and summers off....for now.

Once you realize that three months of summer vacation is just a tradition, you can enjoy the freedom of looking at the year differently. As your family grows and changes, you can arrange the year so that it will work for whatever is going on in your family at that time.

If you have a baby in March, you can take off April without guilt. If relatives are coming for a long-awaited two-week visit in October, you can take that time off to enjoy it with your loved ones. Some homeschoolers take off a few weeks in May to put in their gardens; how about taking off the month of December if you really like to bake, decorate and celebrate the Christmas season? Let yourself break away from the public school calendar you were raised with, and you'll find that all sorts of interesting possibilities arise.

Top Ten Tools for Homeschooling Parents

Every profession requires tools, and homeschooling is no exception. While it's possible to homeschool your children with paper, pencil and a few good books, we homeschoolers tend to be a curious lot, always on the lookout for fun new products to add to our homeschool.

That's why this list does not include curriculum. There are so many great products out there that I could come up with a list a mile long. Instead, I'm looking back on our family's 20 years of homeschooling experience in order to list the top ten tools that made life easier for me as a homeschooling parent.

Let's do this chronologically. We began homeschooling with some books, paper and pencils, and craft supplies. Each day we worked at our kitchen table; we finished our work after an hour or so, and then stacked our books and papers on a little three-shelf unit in our dining room. That didn't last long. As we accumulated more books, our little individual stacks began tipping over, and I got tired of picking up and sorting the mess that resulted. So I bought three plastic boxes with lids; one for me, one for my daughter, and one for my son. They decorated theirs with stickers. Today, we still use **"school boxes,"** as we call them, at our house. They're big enough to hold a stack of books and papers, plus pencils and pens.

All homeschoolers learn that books reproduce like rabbits; soon we were surrounded by books, and it became obvious that we needed **bookshelves**. We began with one simple wooden bookshelf built by my husband, but it eventually became clear that we required something much larger. So we bought an entire wall of bookshelves. With open shelves on the top, and doors covering the bottom two rows of shelves, I could put books on the top shelves and school boxes, games, manipulatives and craft supplies on the shelves behind the doors; our room looked much neater as a result.

The very best part of this major purchase was that we were able to include **a lateral file** in the bookshelf system. It was a great blessing to finally be able to file everything instead of digging around for it. Teacher's keys, achievement test results, invoices for book/curriculum purchases, the children's completed work—all of these had been the object of frantic searches in the past, but that ended once I had a filing system right in our schoolroom. The details of my homeschool filing system can be found in the "On the Home Front" section of this book.

Throughout our homeschool "career," some form of **plan book** kept us on track. At first I recorded what we did each day in a simple datebook. For many years, I bought a teachers' plan book and made lesson plans ahead of time (that's what I did when I was homeschooling all four of my children at one time). These days I use Donna Young's free planning sheets (http://forms.donnayoung.org) for my high schooler, and use a planning sheet I designed specifically for my son, one which includes the goals on his Individualized Education Program (IEP). Even if you're a freewheeling unschooler, keeping a record of what your kids have been doing will be very helpful someday when you're assembling transcripts for them.

Two tools that made our school day easier were the **answering machine** and the **calculator**. The phone always seemed to ring right in the middle of a tough math problem or when someone was reading aloud to me. The answering machine (and later voice mail) allowed us to stay on track. Keeping a calculator at our school table made it easy for me to grade work and figure out GPA's once my children were older.

A **VCR** (and later on, a **DVD player**) was essential to our success in homeschooling. When my younger children were little, educational videotapes kept them occupied while I worked with the older children. In addition, we were able to tap into the wealth of educational videos at our local library for the older children because we had a VCR. Just recently, my daughter and I watched a series on DVD about the Revolutionary War that had been originally produced for cable television (which we do not have). That series came from our public library.

The **computer** has been part of our homeschooling effort for many years. At first we used it for educational games, such as "Oregon Trail" and "Dr. Brain." As the children got older, they wrote their term papers and essays on the computer, which is good practice for college and future jobs. My youngest son, who has developmental delays, learned so much from games that used repetition to help him practice the basics, such as counting and the alphabet. I used the computer to design my teens' high school transcripts, and to make customized worksheets and sight word cards for my youngest.

My most recent acquisition is something I should have bought a long time ago: **a copying machine**. When I think of all the hours I spent over the years collecting dimes and driving to the public library so I could photocopy reproducible worksheets and maps, I can't believe I waited so long. What a blessing it is to have a copier in the house! These days they've come down so much in price that they're irresistible; mine cost less than $200 and is also my printer.

To summarize, here are nine of my top ten tools for homeschoolers:

1) school boxes
2) a wall of bookshelves
3) a lateral file
4) a plan book
5) an answering machine or voice mail
6) a calculator

7) a VCR or DVD player
8) a computer
9) a copying machine

As for the tenth tool, I've saved the best for last. It's **prayer**. We would not be homeschooling today if it weren't for prayer. Panicked prayers, hopeful prayers, and prayers for patience (lots of *those* prayers) —I've prayed for guidance before buying curriculum, before joining homeschool groups and before teaching hormonal teens. All ten tools have been blessings to me as a homeschooling parent, but the most important one by far is prayer!

Oldies But Goodies

Home Grown Kids, A Practical Handbook for Teaching Your Children at Home by Raymond and Dorothy Moore

This book was so integral to my discovery of homeschooling that I sometimes take it for granted that everyone knows about it. But when I talk with today's homeschooling parents, I find that most of them don't know about *Home Grown Kids*. So it's time to introduce a new generation of homeschoolers to this wonderful book.

If you're confused by the wide array of homeschooling books out there, if the ever-increasing number of homeschooling methods overwhelms you, this book will be like a drink of cool water on an intensely hot day. In it, Dr. and Mrs. Moore gently make a case not just for the effectiveness of homeschooling, but for the simplicity of it. No matter how much curriculum you buy and how many books you read, at the end of the day you realize that homeschooling boils down to a caring parent and a child who still has the God-given joy of learning.

The Moores knew that long before this book was published in 1981. From "Note from the Authors" on page 12:

We firmly believe that the greatest teaching talent in the world lies in the warm, responsive and consistent parent whose love makes the needs of his children his highest concern.

While this book promotes homeschooling in the early years (up to age 8 to 10), it also describes a style of parenting of young children that is much needed today. Cuddling without coddling, gentle guidance without harsh discipline or abdication of parental responsibility, and true socialization within the family are all themes of this book. The parent of a newborn will

24

get as much out of it, if not more, than the parent of a five-year-old who is trying to make the school/homeschool decision.

Since this book was first published, much has changed in the school landscape. The Moores discuss the increasing pressure being inflicted on preschoolers and kindergarteners regarding academic pursuits, yet what they were seeing pales in comparison to what's being promoted now: all-day kindergarten, and preschool starting in infancy. Yet their advice still holds true, and will particularly comfort those who have young children and are feeling a lot of peer pressure when it comes to formal preschool. Their description of the warm, nurturing home environment needed for the normal development of children is just what today's parents need.

For the parents of older children, the Moores' detailed discussion of how to determine when a child is ready to read and write is based on research and professional experience, and will make you feel much better about a child who doesn't seem ready at the age the schools say he should be.

The book is laid out in chapters based on children's ages, so you can easily flip to the chapter that describes your child and find plenty of ideas for teaching her in a simple yet effective way.

The final chapter discusses school laws and how they affect homeschooling families. The information is now out of date, of course, yet you can learn a lot about what homeschoolers went through in the 1970s and 1980s that paved the way for the homeschooling movement's incredible growth since then.

If you're looking for encouragement and information that won't overwhelm you, this is the book.

Have You Heard About That Book?

If you stop and listen long enough to the talk among homeschooling moms at Park Day or a homeschool group meeting, you'll probably hear the "buzz" about a certain book or curriculum. There are trends in homeschool circles just as there are in public education, fashion and any other atmosphere that's being marketed to.

Lately, I'm hearing a lot about a book pushing a certain theory of homeschooling. I don't want to name the title, because I haven't read the book yet. I have ordered it, and all I know about it right now is that it is over 600 pages long. This worries me. Not that I think it might be a bad book, because I don't have a clue about its worthiness. What worries me is that most of the talk I've heard about this book is coming from homeschoolers with young children.

Trying to adhere to a philosophy that requires 600 pages to explain sounds like a recipe for burnout to me, especially if the reader is a homeschooling mom with multiple children, including some in diapers. Yet I understand the temptation that each new trend represents. It's that elusive "this might be the one" factor.

When a homeschooling mom hears others raving about the newest trend in homeschooling, she starts thinking, "this might be the one . . . the curriculum that helps me:

- get it all together."
- ensure there are no gaps in my child's education."
- spell out everything we need to do, because I don't have the time to figure all that out."

But no single book could provide me with the thing I didn't have at first that I needed the most: experience. A book might be filled with good ideas, things I could use successfully with my own children, but it couldn't solve all my problems because the author didn't have children identical to mine. I tried different ideas from many books, and many types of curriculum. Some worked for a while, others not at all. A few proved useful for several years. But there's no substitute for experience. The longer you work with your children, the more they teach you about teaching them.

So go ahead and read that new book. Take notes, try things, talk about the book with other moms. But don't expect to find within that book a framework for the next ten years of homeschooling at your house. It's not possible, because no one's situation is just like yours. Instead of putting pressure on yourself to follow the book to the letter, pick and choose what sounds good to you. Put a few of those ideas into action, and see what happens.

If you find the book just doesn't work for you, don't feel bad about the money you spent. If you learn even one good thing from a book, it was worth your time. Besides, at 600 pages plus, if nothing else you can use it as a door stop.

Keys to a Successful Homeschool Convention Experience

Homeschool conventions are exhilarating, informative, interesting and exhausting! I vividly recall my first homeschool convention, even though it was nearly 20 years ago. There was so much to see and learn! I loved being around so many like-minded people who, like me, actually spent their days with their children.

Today, there are far more vendors, workshop presenters and homeschoolers than there were when I began attending conventions. These events can be quite overwhelming, particularly for prospective and new homeschoolers.

The best convention experience is one for which you've prepared yourself. Here are a few keys to success as a convention attendee:

• Study your convention brochure closely ahead of time, so you can choose which sessions you especially want to attend. Highlight them so you can easily refer to them on the day of the convention.

• Be sure to read the speaker biographies. By learning about each speaker, you'll have a better idea of where they're coming from in terms of experience.

• If your husband cannot attend the convention with you, try to arrange carpooling with one or more homeschooling friends. It makes the travel time pass faster, plus you'll be able to compare notes about speakers and sessions on your way home.

• Many homeschool convention organizers don't allow children to attend; they see the event as an educational opportunity for parents. If that's the case at the convention you're attending, be sure to make childcare arrangements far enough ahead of time so that you're all set for the big day.

• If you're a nursing mom, you'll likely be allowed to bring the baby. Be sure you also bring everything your baby needs for a full day of comfort, including extra clothes and diapers, a pacifier to prevent crying during sessions, and an extra blanket in case of excessive air conditioning.

• Pack a cooler with plenty of bottled water, snacks, and your lunch.

• Wear comfy shoes and clothes; you'll be on your feet a lot in the vendor hall.

• Bring a sturdy tote bag (for purchases), a notebook and several pens. (Some people like to bring a wheeled tote or box to drag around, but it's a real nuisance in a crowded vendor hall.)

• Make sure you have cash and/or checks on you; some smaller vendors don't accept credit cards.

Don't forget your convention brochure and the passes or name tags that were sent to you! If you didn't register ahead of time, be sure to arrive early so you have time to register on-site without missing the first session.

Attending Your Homeschool Convention

The big day is here! After finding a parking spot (not always easy at the bigger conventions), you enter the convention's main area to find parents everywhere. Try to find a quiet spot off to the side where you can go through the registration information.

• Study your brochure to see which sessions you want to attend, and then check the building map to locate each of those sessions.

• Check to see if recordings are offered of sessions you can't attend due to schedule conflicts. You can buy them before you go home.

• If you want to attend a session that includes a panel of speakers, make sure there is a moderator. Otherwise, panel discussions have a tendency to be more vague than helpful.

• Are there any vendor workshops for products you might be considering? If so, make a note of when they're held.

• Make a quick sweep of the vendor hall, quickly checking out the booths to see who and what's there, before you buy anything. (Warning: this takes self-control!) While you're at it, pick up free catalogs to add to (or begin) your homeschool catalog collection.

• Remember to turn off your cell phone as soon as you enter a session.

• No one is going to check to see if you took notes, so don't feel you must. But don't think you're going to remember every important thing you hear, because your brain is going to be overwhelmed with good advice today!

• Sometimes speakers offer handouts to help you understand the information they're sharing. Be sure to hang on to these; you may want to refer to them later on.

• If you're not sure you'll stay for an entire session, sit at the back so you can leave without distracting the speaker. The same thing goes if you've brought your baby; a screaming baby in the front row is embarrassing for you and distracting for everyone else.

• Don't be afraid to ask questions of the speaker at the end of the session, or during the session whenever questions are invited. Speakers want to know if they can provide further information; people who are too shy to ask a question can learn from the speaker's response to yours.

• Be sure to thank the speaker at the end of each session. Whether or not they're being paid for their work, they put in a lot of time and effort to share it with you.

• Finally, don't forget to network while you're at the convention. This is your "work," so you'll want to learn from the others in your field. Make conversation with those sitting around you while waiting for a session to start. Ask questions when you need to, and be willing to stop and answer questions from those who need help. The very best part of homeschool conventions is all the wonderful people you'll meet!

Special Tips for the Vendor Hall

The vendor hall is probably the most overwhelming part of a homeschool convention. There are so many great books and resources to look at, and unless you've come with an unlimited budget, so many decisions to make. Get ready to tackle the vendor hall with these tips:

• Leave yourself plenty of time to peruse the vendor hall.
• Check the convention program for vendor coupons that you might be able to use.
• Pray before you buy anything! God will give you guidance, as well as peace about what to buy.
• Sign up for free newsletters and mailing lists.
• Keep an eye out for free samples of curriculum, and pick up every free catalog you can find. If you end up not needing some of them, pass them on to homeschooling friends who weren't able to attend the convention.
• Some of the largest curriculum suppliers (like A Beka and Bob Jones) offer free shipping if you place your order at the convention. But it's crowded and hard to look at their wide variety of curriculum in the vendor hall. Ask if they offer meetings at local motels in your area; they usually offer free shipping at those meetings, and it's a much more relaxing and uncrowded environment in which to make your purchasing decisions. In the meantime, be sure to take their catalogs home so you can study them.

• Step outside for a breath of fresh air every hour or so. A break from the commotion of the vendor hall helps clear your head.

• Go out to your car and regroup at least once during the day. Enjoy the silence while having a cold drink and a snack. Call home to check on everyone. Think about your goals for the rest of the convention. Occasional trips to the car also let you pack away your purchases instead of carrying them around for hours.

• Buy something fun for your children: new construction paper, clay or maybe a special book for each child.

• "Dance with the one that brung ya." If you spend 15 minutes quizzing a vendor about a certain curriculum or resource, then cross the aisle to buy that very product from another vendor because it's a few dollars cheaper there, you have cheated the vendor who spent time talking with you. Be careful not to use vendors in this way. Remember that many of them are homeschooling families trying to earn a living while serving their fellow homeschoolers.

• When exhaustion sets in and you can't think anymore, it's time to go home. But before you go, remember to buy tapes or CDs of the sessions you missed (or the sessions you enjoyed so much that you're going to want to hear them again).

After Your Homeschool Convention

Hopefully, you enjoyed your time at the homeschool convention. Now that you're back home, there's so much to think about: what the speakers said, what you saw in the vendor hall, what you bought and how you want to use it with your children.

Before too much time passes, go through the big stack of papers you brought back. Weed out the sales flyers you don't need, and file those you may want to refer to in the future. Add the catalogs to your collection; you'll want to refer to them in the future when your child finishes a book or program and you need ideas for what to do next.

Think about the speakers whose sessions you attended. What will you do differently in your homeschool because of what you learned from them? Were there some who were especially helpful? You'll want to remember their names for future conventions.

What about the convention itself? Was it well-organized? Was it worth the money you spent to attend it? If you were not happy with the convention, you can always attend a different one in your state, or in a nearby state, next time. Whether you were pleased or displeased with the convention, let the convention organizers know. They need input from attendees so they know how to proceed in organizing future conventions. Often, they will include a survey form in the convention program for just this purpose.

Hopefully, by attending the convention, you came away with renewed enthusiasm for homeschooling. How can you keep that feeling alive long after the convention is over? Listen to the taped sessions when you're in the car. Read books and magazines about homeschooling. Find a support group (if you haven't already done so), attend the meetings and volunteer to run at least one group activity per year. Being with like-minded people is the surest way to keep up your energy and enthusiasm for homeschooling.

Next year, when that convention brochure turns up in your mailbox, you'll find a new group of speakers and sessions that you'll want to hear. By then, with another year's worth of homeschooling under your belt, you'll have an even better idea of how to make your homeschool convention experience a good one.

TEACHING SPECIFIC SUBJECTS

There's plenty of information available about teaching the basic subjects: reading, writing and arithmetic. This section elaborates on subjects beyond the three R's, including life skills, nature, current events, crafts and learning about disabilities.

Does It Count As School?

My son's morning routine is slowly (very slowly) getting faster. It once took him an hour to go to the bathroom, wash his hands and face, brush his teeth and get dressed. Now, several years later, his current "best time" is 15 minutes. That's how it is when you have a child with disabilities. Progress can be very slow in some areas, but you have to keep at it because the child needs to become as independent as he is capable of becoming.

I used to get frustrated by how much time his morning routine ate up, because it cut into our academic time. But after a while I came to realize that dressing himself is an important part of his education. After all, what is the purpose of teaching your child? It's to prepare him for life, and part of life is getting ready every morning for whatever your day will bring.

Like any other child, my son progresses faster in the areas he's interested in. It's not that important to him to get dressed or to read, so his progress in those areas is slow. But he's all about food, so he likes to cook with me. (He would prefer to cook without me, but that's non-negotiable at this point!) Just the other day we made macaroni and cheese for lunch and served it with a fruit salad that he helped assemble. He is a very eager cook, and is good at remembering how to use utensils. When it comes to cooking, he's an "A" student.

But does cooking count as "school"? Sure it does. He is learning a life skill. If he attended public school, he'd be working with therapists who would teach him practical skills like cooking (only they'd call it "food preparation" or "culinary arts.")

Some people would say that activities like self-care and cooking may count as school for a child with developmental disabilities, but for most children, school should be math, reading, history, science, etc. I agree that a well-rounded education includes those subjects (although I think which subjects to include ultimately depends on the parents' personal preferences as well as each child's aptitudes), and I required my other children to study all of them. But that doesn't mean that anything outside of those basic subjects should not count as school.

My teenage daughter and I often walk to the post office or the public library; I count that as her P.E. Last summer she made a quilt and sent it with our church's mission team to Mexico, where it was given to a poor family. I included that on her record as Home Economics and volunteer work (which is now required of many public high school students). Each year, our homeschool group sponsors a card-making/scrapbooking workshop at a local scrapbooking store; that's going down on the books as Art.

When my older children were teens, I put more on their transcripts than just their grades in traditional subjects. I listed my daughter's experience running merchandise tables at concerts to raise money for a pro-life organization, the Christian coffeehouse she started and ran, and her part-time job caring for a neighbor's newborn baby. My son's transcript included the Web site he designed and ran that was written up in *Baseball Weekly*, the mission trips he served on and the non-credit online IT courses he took for fun.

I included these activities on their transcripts because they had learned at least as much (and probably more) from these experiences than they had learned studying traditional subjects. As we later discovered, it certainly didn't hurt to put them on there: my son was accepted at every university to which he applied.

Once you realize that all of your child's activities are learning experiences, you can shed that formal education mentality you were raised with that says only traditional subjects count as school. You realize that almost everything your child learns to do counts as school: reading for pleasure, writing an e-mail to Grandma, making Dad's birthday cake. This continues on into the teenage years. The teen who learns to change the oil in her car, do her own income tax or design and sew her bedroom curtains is doing school.

It doesn't end once the teen becomes an adult. Think of the expectant mother educating herself about the changes in her body and her unborn child as her pregnancy progresses, or the young couple learning all they can about mortgages as they search for their first house. Even the elderly woman studying her options for long-term care facilities is becoming educated in an important subject.

Let's face it: life is school. Everything we do counts as school. Just because we learn something without a book or a teacher or a class does not mean we aren't learning. I figured that out while homeschooling my older children, but it really hit home for me once I understood that my youngest son's school day begins at the bathroom sink. Yes, it counts as school.

Incorporating Nature in Your Homeschool

Here in the Midwest, we're enjoying beautiful spring weather. One of the great things about homeschooling is that we don't have to be cooped up in a school building daydreaming about getting out in the sun. We can use the natural world as our classroom.

There are so many ways to have fun learning about nature. Here are just a few:

Nature hikes

Our support group is blessed with a mom who is a naturalist by trade, and she takes us on nature hikes all year round. Spring is especially exciting, because everything is emerging and changing so quickly. Even if you don't know a naturalist, a visit to a local nature preserve makes for an enjoyable day for the entire family. Many preserves have marked trails, as well as signs explaining the plant and animal life found in the immediate area.

Keeping a nature journal

Each of your children can use a sketchbook or spiral notebook as a nature journal. Find a scenic spot, throw a large blanket on the ground, and hand out the colored pencils. As the children sketch what they see, you can work on a sketch of your own, or just relax for a bit. Bring a small reference book to help identify the trees, plants and animals that your children sketch, or look them up once you get home so everyone can learn more about what they've seen.

It's fun to go back a few weeks later to a place your children sketched and note the changes in the intervening weeks. Of course, another sketch is a great idea. In fact, frequent sketching sessions will produce a wonderful nature journal that will some-day be a keepsake.

Checking things out up close

Take your tribe to a spot with a brook or pond, and bring along a bucket and a magnifying glass or two. Kids love to study the tiny creatures in a bucket of pond water. Leaves and small insects are also fun to examine.

Digital camera = learning tool

Giving your children an inexpensive ($30–40) digital camera will make time spent in nature twice as fun. They can take dozens of shots of flora, fauna and each other, and you won't have to worry about wasting film. Anything that didn't turn out can be deleted at the press of a button.

The good shots can then be used for reports, project fair displays and scrapbooking. If you don't want to print them out, they can be used for a digital scrapbook using the simple art and photo software that probably came with your computer. Don't know how to use that software? Ask your older children (age 7+) or borrow an older child from a friend. It's amazing how quickly they pick up such things.

The digital scrapbook can also be used as a Web page. Many ISP's (Internet service providers) offer free Web pages; check to see if yours is one of them. Think how excited your children will be to email news of their new nature Web page to their friends.

Making time for nature

The hardest part of using nature as a classroom is making time for it. Athletics, recreational classes and for some, a satellite school schedule, often prevent us from getting outside for some unscheduled fun. We're so busy with our obligations that before we know it, summer will be here, and we'll have missed spring.

As keepers of the calendar, we parents have to make time to spend out in nature. That may mean reserving a certain afternoon each week for a nature hike, or even making a date with some homeschooling friends to go with us. For those who feel guilty about taking a few hours to explore the outdoors, consider that it's science, and our children will learn a lot more about it by exploring than by reading about it in a textbook.

Current Events and Homeschooling

When I was in school, back in 19— . . . well, let's just say it was a while back, we had a regular routine our teachers called "Current Events." Every student was required to bring to class a newspaper clipping about something in the news. We would take turns reading our news stories aloud, and then the teacher would interpret them for us.

This, of course, left us with the teacher's view of what was going on in the world, which occasionally caused some youngsters to bring home ideas that opposed those of their parents. I recall my father calling the school more than once to complain about something I was told in school.

One of the many advantages to homeschooling is that you can put your spin on things before your child goes out in to the world. Some people (particularly professional educators) oppose homeschooling for exactly this reason. "Why, if we let their parents teach them," they huff, "these children will think just like their parents."

That statement is silly. First of all, why shouldn't we exercise our right as parents to tell our children about the world? It's our job. And second, how many children agree with their parents 100% of the time anyway? Give the kids a little credit for being able to think.

Homeschooling is an ideal environment for learning about current events. The publisher of our local newspaper is always asking readers to donate money to finance putting newspapers in all the local classrooms, but do schoolchildren even have time during the day to read those papers? Our home always has a current newspaper in it, and we often talk about current events in our family.

At times over the years, we also subscribed to *God's World* weekly newspapers. They were great for getting my children into the habit of paying attention to what's going on outside of our area; like most kids, mine loved receiving something with their name on it in the mail.

Current events take on a greater immediacy when you can stop what you're doing and watch events unfold on television, as we homeschoolers can. When Los Angeles was hit by an earthquake in 1994, the children (then ages 1–11) and I skipped our usual schoolwork routine and watched the coverage all day on television. We had a special interest in what was going on because my sister lives there, but even after we found out she was safe, we continued to watch, fascinated by the reports from various parts of the city, the scientific explanations of what had happened under the earth's surface, and the amazing video of the damage.

When terrorists struck the U.S on September 11, 2001, we were glued to both the television and the Internet in an effort to find out what was going on. The terrible insecurity of that day was eased somewhat by having all of our children home safe with us.

When my oldest daughter was doing high school at home, I combined current events with expository writing by assigning her to write a weekly current events essay. I chose each week's topic from whatever was in the news at the time. She was in her last year of high school during the controversial 2000 presidential election, so there was no lack of subjects to write about. The electoral college, the role of the Supreme Court, how ballots are designed...you name it, I assigned her to write about it. She also wrote about gasoline prices, nuclear weapons, terrorism and a myriad of other topics.

I usually assigned the essay topic on Monday, which gave her all week to research her topic using newspapers, magazines and the Internet. The essay was due Friday afternoon, and after I graded it, we'd discuss what she learned. We had some thought-provoking conversations, because she is a very opinionated person (can't figure out where that came from . . .). I put her brother through the same routine when he did high school at home. When he was in college, his essay-writing background served him well: he graduated magna cum laude.

Whether your children are young or nearly grown, you'll find that studying current events becomes an important part of their education. Thanks to the Internet, a quick Yahoo or Google search can generate plenty of primary sources of information. If you make current events a regular part of your homeschool, you'll find that you and your children will become very well-informed about what's going on in the world.

Making Friends and Projects with a Homeschool Sewing Class

Sewing classes are a great way for homeschooled girls to get to know each other while learning a useful skill. A while back, I offered a series of three hand-sewing classes to a homeschool group we had recently joined, and it resulted in friendships developing between my daughter and several other girls.

I chose hand-sewing over machine-sewing for two reasons. First, machine-sewing requires plenty of room for tables and electrical outlets for all those sewing machines. I wanted to offer the class in my home, and we don't have a room large enough for that. Second, I've taken enough machine-sewing classes to know that they aren't conducive to conversation because of the noise of the machines, and the concentration that using a sewing machine requires. I wanted to provide an opportunity for the girls to sit and talk, so hand-sewing was the best option.

I put a notice in the homeschool group's fall newsletter, offering three two-hour classes, one weekday afternoon per month during September, October and November. I limited each class to six participants, so that I could provide individual help to those who might need it. Keeping the classes small also made for a more intimate group, which I hoped would be helpful for getting even the shyest girls to talk.

My daughter was 11 then, so I suggested an age range for participants of 9–13 years of age. I asked that each girl bring a small sewing kit, consisting of scissors, a small package of hand-sewing needles, a small package of straight pins, and a pincushion. I charged $5 per person per class, to cover the expense of materials and refreshments.

The classes filled up quickly. As each class day approached, I made up sample projects in order to provide the girls

44

with a visual of what they would be making. I multiplied the supplies and amount of fabric I used for each project by six, and then set out to buy the supplies so that I could assemble kits ahead of time for each girl. I used discount coupons from fabric and craft store sale flyers in order to keep the final cost under $5 per person.

For the September class, the girls made small reversible table runners. They sewed together two fabric rectangles, one of a bright fall print and the other of muslin, using a simple running stitch. To the muslin side they then ironed leaves, which I had made ahead of time using red, yellow, orange, green and brown fabrics cut in the shape of leaves, with iron-on adhesive on the backs.

It was a simple project, but the girls were delighted with the results. The two hours passed quickly. Though the girls were quiet at first, they soon relaxed, and before long, there was plenty of giggling and chatter. A couple of the girls were experienced at hand-sewing and finished early, but their willingness to share their experience by helping the others meant that everyone was busy almost to the end of the class. New friendships were made that day, and it was fun to watch.

In October the girls made sachets. Before class, I assembled kits that included teddy-bear shapes I'd cut out of purple flannel, a piece of lavender lace for an inset, lavender and pink variegated embroidery thread, pom-poms for eyes, nose and mouth, and gardenia-scented potpourri for the stuffing. It took the full two hours for the girls to handstitch the lace over a hole cut in the front of the bear, stitch the bear pieces together, and fill the bear with potpourri. With little time remaining, each girl quickly glued the pom-poms to her bear's face, and then tied a purple satin ribbon in a bow around its neck. Potpourri could be seen through the circular lace inset on the front of the bear, an effect that made the sachets look more difficult to make than they really were. The girls were quite impressed with their finished projects, and celebrated with cookies and lemonade.

For the November class, in addition to the sewing kit, each girl was required to bring an 11.5- or 18-inch tall doll, similar to a Barbie or an American Girl doll. Fortunately, everyone brought the latter. The smaller doll is much harder to sew for, but I included that size in case someone didn't have the larger doll. But everyone did, so we set out to make Christmas skirts for the dolls.

The girls used rectangles of green or red velvet to make the skirts. Using fabric chalk, I had already marked sewing lines. The girls sewed the short edges together for the side seam, then folded over and stitched a casing along the long edge. They ran elastic through that casing for the gathered waist of the skirt, and put the skirts on their dolls to adjust for a perfect fit.

After a quick break for cookies and juice, the real fun began. Using fabric glue, the girls arranged and attached a variety of trims, beads and other decorations to the skirts. There were red, green and white lace bows, gold and silver baubles, and gold and silver braid to choose from. The braid, when glued along the bottom of the skirts, covered up the raw edge of the hem so that hand-hemming was not required.

The result was six well-dressed dolls, proudly presented by the creators of their elegant Christmas skirts. The girls excitedly discussed plans for displaying their dolls in their finery at upcoming Christmas gatherings.

Thanks to the sewing classes, my daughter made several new friends, and I got acquainted with their moms. My daughter had so much fun that some months later, she offered a few informal sewing classes to a friend in the neighborhood. As American women learned decades ago from quilting bees and sewing circles, having a project to keep your hands busy makes talking with new friends a little easier.

If you'd like to plan sewing or other craft classes for your homeschool group, here are some tips to make the job easier:

• Pick a class day when your schedule is open, because the class may run long.

• Plan seasonal projects that are appropriate for the class dates.

• Set limits on age and number of participants that suit your purpose.

• Set a sign-up deadline so that you have enough time to get the right quantity of supplies.

• Send confirmation letters or emails to those who sign up.

• Once you have a head count, buy the amount of fabric and supplies you need, plus a little extra in case someone makes a mistake and needs another piece of fabric or elastic.

• Prepare a sample, writing down each step of the project as you make it.

• Assemble kits in plastic bags ahead of time; prepare the materials so that the project can be finished in the time allotted (ex. measure and cut out pieces, mark seams, measure and cut elastic, etc.). The girls can take their finished projects home in the plastic bags.

• Include a kit for yourself, so you can demonstrate each step as you lead the class.

Teaching Your Children About Disabilities

Disabled children are much more visible in today's society than they were in the past, when they were often hidden away in hospitals and institutions. Today, they are seen regularly in public places because ours is a much more enlightened culture when it comes to the rights and needs of the disabled.

Children in formal schools can become personally acquainted with disabled children because of the educational policy of inclusion, or mainstreaming. The purpose of the policy is to breed acceptance for the disabled among those who are not disabled. Of course, it doesn't always work out as planned; some children can be quite cruel to those with disabilities. But the intent of inclusion is a good one.

Homeschooled children are not affected by inclusion, so it's up to their parents to teach them about people with disabilities. This is easier to do if there is a special needs child in your neighborhood, church or homeschool group. But whether or not you personally know a special needs child, there are great resources* that will help you explain various disabilities to your children, and help them understand that disabled children are more like them than different from them. Kids with disabilities like to have fun, they like to learn and they love to hang out with their friends. The difference is that all these things can be much harder for them because of their disabilities.

Teaching your children about disabilities may not seem like a necessity to you. After all, there are already a lot of subjects for your children to learn about. But as the parent of a disabled child, I must tell you that how you and your children react to a disabled child greatly affects that child and his family. A good reaction can be a blessing, while a negative reaction can hurt tremendously. Teach your children about disabilities, and they won't hurt their friends . . or embarrass you out in public, either.

After our son Josh's birth and hospitalization, it took several months before I got to the point where I could take all four kids (and Josh's apnea monitor) out by myself, but once I did, my kids were overjoyed to see their friends at field trips and other outings. Some days it took every ounce of energy I could muster, but I took them places as often as I could. By that point, they were more than ready to get out of the house and have some fun.

I recall that some people reacted awkwardly to seeing our new baby, but others reacted with joy when they saw us. If and when you have an opportunity to meet up with someone with a disabled child, be sure to prepare your children by explaining the child's disability ahead of time. If they have some understanding of what's going on, they'll be more comfortable around the family, which will make the family more comfortable, too.

One mom recalled how hurt her eldest child was when his friend told him that his new baby sister was funny-looking. The boy was naturally quite protective of the baby, and a comment like that cut deeply. It would have been easier to take had the comment come from a preschooler, but unfortunately it came from an older child.

Consider your children fortunate if they should have the opportunity to make friends with a child with disabilities. Simply by their existence, these children teach others about love, mercy, and kindness, and help them develop a servant's heart. Kids with a special needs sibling have the chance to develop these virtues on a daily basis; your children can develop them, too, if you give them the opportunity to befriend a disabled child.

Your children will probably ask you how kids come to have special needs and why a loving God would allow this. I don't think there's any better explanation than the Biblical story of the blind man in the book of John:

> *And as Jesus passed by, he saw a man which was blind from his birth.*
> *And his disciples asked him, saying, Master, who did sin, this man, or his parents, that he was born blind?*
> *Jesus answered, Neither hath this man sinned, nor his parents: but that the works of God should be made manifest in him. (John 9:1–3, KJV)*

Other translations quote Jesus at the end of that passage as saying, "so that the works of God might be displayed in him," or, "in his life." Which works of God would those be? The works of God in our hearts that occur when we are given the opportunity to serve people like the blind man, people who have disabilities. In other words, those works can be displayed in your children's behavior toward disabled children—helping them, making friends with them, including them—once you have taught them about disabilities.

Keep in mind that it's easier for children (and adults) to warm up to an infant or small child with disabilities. But what happens when a new family moves into your neighborhood or joins your homeschool group, and their disabled child is not a cute little baby, but an older child or even a teen who exhibits odd behavior?

Consider this another learning experience for your children. If your child has been homeschooled for most or all of his life, he may never have known anyone with disabilities, and his reactions may reflect that.

I recall a homeschool bowling outing we attended with several families, including one whose children had apparently never seen a child with Down syndrome. While Josh was bowling, he noticed two older girls staring at him, and he became a little annoyed. At first he scowled at them, but when they continued to stare at him, he began goofing off (making silly faces and strange sounds), which is what he does when he's uncomfortable around someone.

They reacted by staring even harder at him. I finally sent them back to their own lane, but I wondered what, if anything, I should have said to them. I didn't know them or their mother, so I felt it best to leave the issue alone, but I still wish they had know a little bit about Down syndrome. It would have made my son (and me!) a lot more relaxed that day.

This is an issue you'll want to think about, because these days, an increasing number of parents are pulling their special needs children out of the public schools in order to homeschool them. It's possible that a new family with a disabled child could join your support group. By preparing your child ahead of time, you'll pave the way for your child's inner growth as well as a friendly welcome for the disabled child.

*Here are some resources you can use to teach your children about special needs:

For Children:
Where's Chimpy? by Berniece Rabe is a favorite at our house. It's a great book for young children, a picture book about a little girl's search for her stuffed monkey. Published by Albert Whitman Company (http://www.albertwhitman.com)

(Note: Albert Whitman Company specializes in children's books about disabilities)

Markie and the Hammond Cousins and *Ricky and the Hammond Cousins* by Wanda M. Yoder are companion books that tell the story of how a group of children learn to relate to children with disabilities. Published by Christian Light Publications.

For Parents:

To understand what parents experience when they are given a child with special needs, be sure to read this article by my friend Bobbi Bandy:

http://www.lutheransforlife.org/Life_Issue_Info/Family _Living/A_Life_Not_Like_Any_Other.htm

Here's the book she wrote about her son Rob, *The Dance Goes On*:

http://www.christianbook.com/Christian/Books/product?it em_no=734082&kw=734082&en=froogle&p=1013824

Do you have a friend who needs support as she homeschools a special needs child? Send her to NATHHAN (National Challenged Homeschoolers Associated Network):

http://www.nathhan.com

TEACHING TECHNIQUES AND IDEAS

You'll find ideas for developing patience, explaining concepts, solving problems, testing your children and homeschooling a child with special needs in this section.

Patience

When people find out that I homeschool my children, they almost always say something along the lines of, "I could never do that. You must be a really patient person."

Most of the time, I respond that I wasn't patient when I started (my husband can vouch for that), but that my patience developed over the years. I don't go into too much detail because I've discovered that most of these people don't really want to know how to become more patient. They're just grabbing onto the first excuse they can think of to explain why they can't (read: don't want to) homeschool their children.

But the question of patience is an interesting one. My mother-in-law has commented many times that she is amazed by my patience with my children. Please don't be fooled by that; I am not always patient with them. In fact, in certain situations, I have to send myself into time-out so I don't wring someone's neck (usually that someone is a teenager). But I do think that I have more patience than I once did, thanks to many years of trying to get my children to understand concepts and ideas because I want to help them learn. It is so rewarding to see the light go on when a challenging idea becomes understandable. That light won't go on if I'm breathing down my child's neck.

Early on, when trying to explain a concept to one of my children, I would start asking questions to make them think. But soon I'd find myself clueing them in on the answers right away because I got tired of waiting for them to say the right thing. Of course, they weren't learning anything when I fed them the answer. The next time the subject came up, I could see that they didn't know anything more this time than before I'd explained it. The answer wouldn't make sense to them unless it came from their understanding, not my spoon-feeding method.

So I learned to wait for them to catch on. When they'd ask me a question, I'd answer it, and come back with a few of my own to make them think a little harder. Then instead of coaching them to the correct answers, I just waited. Sooner or later, they'd figure it out.

After we'd been homeschooling for several years, I was given a new opportunity for learning patience: our son Josh was born with Down syndrome. In most areas, it took him far longer to learn things than it had taken his siblings. He didn't crawl until he was 1, and didn't start walking until 21 months. He'd been in physical therapy since he was tiny, but I'm not sure whether he would have crawled or walked later without it. What I've seen with him is that he will not do something until he is ready, and in this way he is much like his brother and sisters. He is my graduate study in the School of Patience.

For example, he did not become toilet-trained until he was seven. We tried coaxing, training and occasional forcing him to use the toilet starting at age three. We bought him potty books and a video. We even tried bribing him with M&M'S®. But he wasn't ready yet.

When he was five or six, he started using the toilet once a day or so. When he was successful, he would make the general announcement ("Poo-poo! Poo-poo!"), and cheering and applause would break out from every corner of the house. Still, it would be well over a year before he could go without diapers all the time (and probably two or three years before he stopped demanding M&M'S® after each successful bathroom visit).

What a golden opportunity toilet-training him was for teaching us about patience. Nothing we did spurred him on. But when he figured it out, the triumph was all his.

This concept also holds for children who are not mentally delayed or disabled. For example, when a teenager finally figures out quadratic equations, it's his victory. Sure, Mom and Dad have answered numerous questions, most more than once, and each was a stone in the path leading up to the day when he figured out the concept. But he's the one who succeeded in grasping the concept.

Now imagine if each time he'd asked his parents a question, they'd responded with a sigh, or worse, with anger ("How many times do I have to explain this to you?"). That would have discouraged him from asking any more questions, and it would have taken that much longer for him to pick up the concept. Or, he might never have figured it out. How sad if he was just one question away from understanding, but was afraid to ask that question.

Some kids need to ask more questions than others, and that can be very wearing on the homeschooling parents who spend their days coming up with the answers. It's important for us to remember that each question brings the child closer to the point of understanding. Allowing him to reach that point, no matter how many questions it takes, is something that can't be done in formal school, because the logistics of teaching a group don't permit it. That's one of the reasons homeschooling is so successful: the child can move at his own pace, with the support of an adult who will answer his questions and patiently wait for him to "get it," so that he can move on. A classroom teacher can't possibly do that with a roomful of students.

The longer you homeschool, the better you get at patiently answering the same question many times. You also get better at waiting for the answers to questions you've asked in order to make your child come to a certain conclusion. Your patience in such matters greatly benefits each of your children.

I wish I could tell you that the patience you develop over years of homeschooling translates into more patience in other areas of your life, but I can't. Ask my son Peter, who had to keep me calm throughout 90 minutes in line waiting for him to get his ID at college registration ($26,000 a year, and they can only afford one ID machine?). Or you could ask those people who drive in front of me at 10 mph below the speed limit; I'm on them like a cheap suit. I guess it's going to take more than years of homeschooling to make me into a totally patient person.

Rewind, Please

One of the best things about watching a movie on a VCR is that if you miss something, you can pause the machine, rewind the movie a bit, and play it back, in slow-motion if necessary, so you can see or hear what you missed. You can do the same thing with a DVD player. What a convenience that is, especially for those of us whose ability to see or hear is showing signs of age!

The willingness to pause and rewind is essential when you are teaching your child. If she doesn't understand something, don't keep plowing ahead with the lesson. Even if you feel the pressure to do so because you're trying to keep up with a lesson plan, or you want her to stay at grade level in a certain subject, moving ahead when she doesn't understand is counter-productive. Instead, you need to:

PAUSE...REWIND...RESUME PLAY (IN SLOW MOTION, IF NECESSARY)

PAUSE: stop as soon as you realize there's a problem. Don't get angry or frustrated. It's not your child's fault that she doesn't understand, any more than it's your fault when you can't hear something in a movie. Instead, talk to her and let her express her frustration a bit. Try to figure out where you lost her.

REWIND: go back to a place where you know your child understood everything. If it's math, go back a few concepts. If it's a formal lesson book in any subject, go back a few pages. If it's reading, go back a page or two.

PLAY (IN SLOW MOTION, IF NECESSARY): Start re-viewing the things she already knows, watching carefully for the beginning signs of difficulty as you lead up to the part she didn't understand. Once you reach the trouble spot, present the material again. Cover the material slowly; proceed cautiously.

Hopefully, this review will help her understand. But if it doesn't, you may need to change tactics. Take some time to review the basic concepts of the subject. Have her reread the chapter leading up to the part she didn't understand.

Come up with alternate ways of presenting the material. You may even need to look for supplemental materials to help her get over this area of difficulty.

If none of those remedies work, accept that sometimes you simply have to stop. Take a breather. Pick up where you left off in a few days or weeks. Often, things will have improved by then.

But whatever you do, don't keep forging ahead. We rewind parts of movies because we want to understand what's going on, and what is yet to come. Likewise, we want our children to understand what they're learning, so they can build on it as they progress. So when your child doesn't understand something the first time around, remember to

PAUSE...REWIND...RESUME PLAY (IN SLOW MOTION, IF NECESSARY).

Boosting Problem-Solving Skills

For me, one of the joys of homeschooling has been finding really good resources. Over the years, we have used some excellent products that the kids and I all enjoyed.

Most of these resources were aimed at a specific age range. But there was one series that we have used since the kids were small, and continued to use right into the teen years, and that is the group of three workbooks that make up the Critical Thinking Activities series by Dale Seymour Publications.

These workbooks contain a wide variety of written activities, including pencil puzzles, dot designs, logic problems, and Venn diagrams. The purpose of these activities is to help children develop problem-solving and higher-level thinking skills.

Each book is divided into three sections: Patterns, Imagery and Logic. In the first book, for grades K–3, the Patterns section includes simple number problems, shape patterns (which shape comes next?), and number trains. The Imagery section includes finding and coloring specific shapes, finding and matching identical pictures amongst a group of very similar ones, and simple cut and glue puzzles. The logic section includes Venn diagrams and some simple true-false problems. These are just a few examples; there is a wide range of activities in each section.

The other workbooks, for grades 4–6 and 7–12, have more challenging versions of similar problems as those in the first book. They also have symmetry activities, designs to plot on graph paper, and logic problems (sets of statements with a chart you fill in with X's and dots to solve a problem).

Kids like these books because they're fun, and a painless way to learn. There are many more reasons for homeschooling parents to like them:

• Within each book, problems are labeled with one, two or three triangles (the more triangles, the harder the problem), so it's easy to determine what's appropriate for the level your child is at.

    • The books are reproducible (I made copies for my older children; now my younger children write in the books), but can also be used as workbooks.

    • The books are very reasonably priced (around $19 retail, but available at a discount from some homeschool catalogs), considering the variety of problems in them, and the fact that there are between 170 and 190 pages in each.

    •The answers are in the back, and arranged so that you can correct easily and quickly.

    • These books are wonderful for children who are not math wizards; the activities teach them how to think logically.

    Should you be lucky enough to find an unsullied copy of one of these books for a good price at a used curriculum sale, snap it up. Even if your children are too old for it, one of your homeschooling friends will be thrilled to get it.

Testing Your Homeschooled Child

This week my daughter and I have reserved two mornings to spend some time alone together.

We'll probably pick up some hot chocolate from McDonald's on our way to the public library, where I've already reserved a study room. There we'll spend two hours in peace and quiet. I plan to bring a book I've been reading, while she keeps busy with something I'm bringing for her: the California Achievement Test.

I look at testing as something that breaks up our routine and gives me a little quiet time away from the house. I try to make it comfortable for both of us, though as far my daughter is concerned, any morning without her math book is a good one.

Advantages of Testing

In my state, we're not required to test our children, and over the years I haven't tested mine very often. But I find occasional testing useful for my own purposes. It gives me a rough idea of where my children are at in several different subject areas compared to public school children. This information will be useful if my children ever have to go to public school (let's hope not!), and it also reveals if they are behind in any area.

Another reason testing (especially for the first time) is worthwhile is that it can give both parent and child a boost of self-confidence. My two older children were tested for the first time when they were seven and eight. Their scores were terrific, and that confirmed to us that we were doing the right thing by homeschooling.

Testing on Your Own

I'm homeschooling just my two younger children now, and I test them separately using materials I order over the phone or by mail. I obtained the test my daughter is about to take at http://www.setontesting.com. I rent tests for my son (who is developmentally disabled) from Home School Legal Defense Association (www.hslda.org). Testing him at home works especially well, because he is easily distracted in a group setting.

That doesn't mean I am against group testing. The first two times I tested my older children, they were part of a large group of homeschoolers, and it worked out very well. In fact, they thought it was great fun, and so did I. (You can read more about that experience in the "Covering All the Bases" section of this book.)

Preparing for the Test

No matter how I test my children, I don't prepare them much because I don't want to teach to the test the way the schools do; it seems to me like that skews the scores. I just show them ahead of time how to fill in the answer sheet. I also study the test first so that I have an idea of how to administer it.

For older kids, I also explain test-taking strategies such as skipping the questions that are way too hard in order to have enough time to finish the easier ones first. Of course, what strategy to teach depends on how the test was designed. If there's no penalty for wrong answers, I tell them to go back and attempt the problems that are extremely difficult if there's time remaining after they've finished the easier questions.

When we go to the library to test, we bring a few new pencils, a timer, some scratch paper and a good book or magazine for me to read during the actual testing. I don't allow my children to ask questions about the content of a test, but they can ask questions about the actual testing experience, such as how much time they have left on a section, and whether they should turn the page.

In the case of college admissions tests like the ACT or SAT, their Web sites include practice tests that explain to test-takers how their tests will be scored and what strategy to use. Of course, parents are not allowed to administer the actual test; their involvement is limited to signing them up to take the test locally* and going over the practice test with their children ahead of time.

Test Results

Whether you test your children on your own or in a group, the scores can be sent directly to you. They arrive fairly quickly; once they do, you can spend some time assessing your children's strengths and weaknesses, and determining the focus of your homeschooling efforts.

If you notice any areas where they're uniformly behind, you'll know which subjects should be at the top of your shopping list the next time you buy books and resources.

It's likely that your children's test scores will be above average. Recent studies indicate that homeschooled children score an average of 15–30 percentage points higher than their public school peers.

No matter how your children score, try to look at test scores as guidelines for you rather than an assessment of them. Test scores are not the final word; they are only meant to give you a general idea of how your children are doing. You're with your children more than anyone else, so you already have a pretty good idea of each one's abilities. Ultimately, test scores are just one small piece of the puzzle.

* go to http://www.actstudent.org/index.html (ACT) or http://www.collegeboard.com/testing (SAT)

Homeschooling a Child
with Special Needs

After you've been homeschooling for a while, you become comfortable in your role as teacher. Working with your children year after year brings you to an understanding of how they learn and what to expect of them. As the years pass, you witness a fairly steady progression of increasing skills, a growing desire to work independently, and less direct instruction needed from you, their teacher, as they grow.

I found that to be true of my first three children. Homeschooled from birth, really, they taught me that if you provide books, resources, relaxed instruction, and a willingness to answer their questions, they'll do the rest.

But it doesn't work like that with Josh. He has Down syndrome, which makes learning harder for him than it was for the others. He has the curiosity to learn, but his disabilities get in his way. As his mom and his teacher, I've learned to change my expectations and my teaching style in order to help him progress. Homeschooling him is different than homeschooling his older siblings, and both of us are learning many new things.

New Expectations

The first thing you learn when you have a child with special needs is to adjust your expectations. My older children taught me to expect regular improvement, but with Josh, improvement can take a long time. Picture long plateaus with the occasional rise coming between them. For example, my older children learned their letters and numbers through the repetition that occurs naturally in life. When they saw words and numbers in books or on street signs and asked what they were, they remembered my responses to their questions. But my youngest rarely remembered the responses; he didn't even start asking the questions until he was eight or nine years old.

The older children made gradual progress toward working independently, but my youngest cannot stay on task unless someone is right there with him. Just washing his hands often requires supervision and encouragement. Independence is something quite a ways down the road, and it will be hard-won.

When at a park or a museum, my older children could be expected to stay in the area, so they had a lot of autonomy while there. Josh, however, is a runner, and will take off if we don't stay right with him. Even playing outside, where so much learning occurs, is something that requires supervision in his case. While we take him outside as often as we can, those times are limited by the availability of someone to police him.

A New Teaching Style

As my expectations changed, I realized that the teaching style I had developed while homeschooling the older children also had to change. When working with them, I could assume they understood me if they didn't ask many questions. But my son isn't proactive that way. I have learned to question him regularly about things we have read or done. If he doesn't respond in a way that shows understanding, I have to come up with a different way to present the material.

I also need to play more games with him than I did with the others. I used educational games as an occasional tool with my older children, but with my son it has become an integral part of our time together each day. He is very competitive, with a strong desire to learn whatever it takes to win the game. Thanks to him, we have amassed a large collection of number and letter games, all of them well-worn by now.

With the older three, I used phonics to assist them as they taught themselves to read. That was how I learned to read, and it fit all of us. But my son has severe speech delays, so sounding out words is much harder for him than it was for his siblings.

Sight reading works better for him, so I've learned to use a technique I was never crazy about before, because in this case, it works.

While I spent a lot of one-on-one time with each of my children, I can never put in enough "face time" with Josh. Getting right in his face to work with him has been the most effective way of teaching him since he was tiny. He is easily distracted; I need to stay right with him and keep him on track. We accomplish a lot if I am "in his face" most of the time.

Trying New Methods

My teaching style changed after I adjusted my expectations of my son. I could not rest on what I had learned by teaching the others. As I saw that the way I was used to doing things wasn't helping him, I followed his cues to develop new methods.

For instance, in order to count verbally, he first needed to fully understand the concept of each number. While counting trucks on the highway or birds in the backyard solidified the concept of numbers for my older children, I had to find many more ways to do that for our little guy. We used plastic numbers and manipulatives. We counted everything we used, and never put the crayons back in the box without counting them first. We played number lotto, board games and hopscotch. If it had to do with number concepts, we tried it.

What finally did the trick for him was the board game "Trouble." The two of us played that game at least once a day for over a year. He'd carry the box into his dad's home office, and they'd play at least one daily game. He'd accost the teenagers as they arrived home from work with the greeting, "Trouble?" And after countless games of "Trouble" with everyone in the family, something clicked, and he finally figured out the numbers one to six.

Another area in which I needed to change was how I looked at workbooks. Josh really enjoys them. He displays such a sense of accomplishment when he finishes a page. The older children would use a workbook once and then move on. But when my youngest son finishes a workbook, he won't necessarily remember everything he learned from it. So we work our way through two or three copies of some of them. By the second time, he has usually mastered a few new concepts and finds it easier, which really encourages him (and me). We worked through Rod and Staff's six-workbook preschool series twice. These days, I photocopy the pages of higher-level workbooks; he has done some pages five times or more. He beams when he completes a page correctly.

Using the help of a professional was another area that required me to change. I never needed or wanted the help of others when homeschooling the older three children. But when your child has special needs, therapists can provide necessary guidance for you as your child's teacher. On the recommendation of a homeschooling friend, we hired a very experienced, pro-homeschooling speech therapist when Josh was little. In addition to working with him, she taught me how to reinforce his speech sessions at home. She also evaluated him periodically, and answered my questions about his progress.

Testing and IEP's

Probably the biggest change in my teaching style has been a new willingness to work using testing and Individualized Education Programs (IEP's), which are very specific lesson plans. Although I used achievement tests with my older children a few times, I never relied on them for anything but encouragement. With my youngest, however, test results are my guide to what to do next with him.

The tests I give my son are not achievement tests, but skills tests, which break down each skill found in human development into single steps. By finding out where he is developmentally, I can see what skill is next in each area, and direct my teaching efforts accordingly.

At first, my husband and I hired an educational psychologist to do the testing. But our son didn't warm to this man. In fact, he became very withdrawn upon meeting the psychologist. We had never seen our son act like that before. Interestingly, after the session was over, he went back to being his usual chipper self. But we could see that his reaction to this man affected his test responses negatively.

The testing session cost us $400. Since testing is recommended every three months, we decided to find a less costly and more successful alternative. A little research revealed that we could rent the same test from the Home School Legal Defense Association (HSLDA) for less than $30. Now I test him myself, and use the results to design his IEP.

When I first heard about IEP's, they sounded way too structured for me. Like many homeschoolers, I had become a less structured teacher over the years. But working with my son made me see that I needed goals for him, since he didn't take the initiative or make progress as easily as his siblings had. We needed specific areas of development to work toward. The tests showed us what those were, and the IEP's established a game plan for reaching them.

The IEP simply lists the goals we're working on, and the activities and resources we'll need to get there. I update the IEP every three or four months. In some areas my son makes steady progress, but in others we have to repeat steps. I'm learning to work at his speed, so it can be slow going. On the other hand, because of the effort he makes and the time it takes him, his victories are especially sweet.

Help from Older Siblings

My older children have helped my youngest as he learns. We've taught them to do things with him in specific ways so that they can add to the daily repetition he needs in many areas. They help him set the table at times, but they know to make him count out the silverware. When they play games with him, they know just how much to help him without letting him coast. He adores his siblings, and is always willing to work with them.

When they were younger, and I was homeschooling all four of them, things got pretty hectic. It was hard bouncing back and forth between teenagers doing trigonometry, a 3rd grader learning multiplication, and a seven-year-old who was still having trouble distinguishing between the numbers 2 and 3. Often, I worked with one older child while another played with Josh. Later, they would trade places. In this way, our son got lots of attention and the older ones still got their one-on-one time with me.

Asking the older children to occasionally cover an assignment on the IEP made it easier to accomplish everything planned for a given day. But siblings of children with special needs already make a lot of sacrifices, so I always tried not to overdo it. They needed to keep a balance in their lives between helping their brother and doing the things that were important for them.

The Benefits of Homeschooling Don't Change

Homeschooling my son with Down syndrome is different from homeschooling the others, and yet the benefits are the same. He receives plenty of the one-on-one attention he sorely needs, which would not be possible in the public school setting. He enjoys close relationships with his siblings, thanks to all the time they've spent together over the years. He misses out on the opportunity to learn bad behavior from the kids at school (something we've heard is common among Down syndrome children, who are often talented mimics). He also misses out on the teasing that children with disabilities often suffer from in school, as well as the pity of well-meaning others.

At home, he is one of the gang, learning new things every day, just as his two oldest siblings did, and his big sister still does. And I am learning too: new techniques, new resources, more patience. Homeschooling continues to be a constant source of learning for all of us.

For more information about homeschooling children with special needs, contact:

NATHHAN (National Challenged Homeschoolers Associated Network)
P.O. Box 39
Porthill, ID, 83853

On the Web, go to www.nathhan.com.

COVERING ALL THE BASES

It takes guts to homeschool. When you choose to teach your children at home, you demonstrate a lack of faith in the other avenues of education that are available to you and your family. Since most of us were educated in the public school system and were raised to believe it was the fount of most knowledge, choosing to reject it in favor of homeschooling is seen as a pretty radical decision in our society.

It would be ideal if you came into this job with a complete theory of education in your head: what it entails, how it should be done, how to measure success. In fact, some parents do begin homeschooling with a personal philosophy of how to educate their children all ready and waiting. Sometimes, it's what made them decide to homeschool their children in the first place.

For many parents, however, the decision to homeschool is not one that was thought out for years in advance. It is often precipitated by a child's negative experiences in formal school or social pressure from church or family; sometimes, it's the sudden realization that God is leading them in that direction, even though it wasn't what they would have chosen otherwise.

In such situations, it would sure be helpful to have a personal philosophy of education to rely on for direction. Rest assured, that will come in time. It will take time to think about your own education and to remember its pluses and minuses. Taking the time to look closely at your children, paying special attention to how each one learns, what their interests are and how well you relate to each of them will also help. Most important of all, what you learn from the successes and failures that you experience while teaching your children will become the basis for your personal theory of education. That will definitely take a while.

In the meantime, it helps to find out what other parents have learned about learning. The following section describes the philosophy I developed while homeschooling my children for the past two decades. In it, you'll find some thought-provoking questions to ask yourself, as well as information that will help you make the necessary decisions of what subjects are important for your children to learn. There's also a brief discussion of achievement testing, and what it can do for you and your children.

You may not agree with everything I report in this section; that's all right. What's important is that it gets you thinking about your children, how they learn, and how you can provide them with a warm, loving educational environment tailored to their needs.

Whether they're beginners or veterans, most homeschoolers sometimes find themselves wondering:

Are we covering all the bases?

What are the bases anyway?

How do I know if we're doing everything we're supposed to be doing?

Are we covering the right subjects at the right times?

Are we using the right materials?

Are my kids doing OK?

Within these questions lies the fear that homeschooling might produce children who are really weak in some areas. Without guidelines about what to teach, won't there be lots of gaps in our children's education? Somewhere there must be a list of things to know that we can check off as we go along.

What are the Bases?

The idea that there is One Body of Knowledge (the bases) that must be passed on to each child is a fallacy. Think of all the things there are to learn in this incredible world of ours. No human being could possibly learn it all! Albert Einstein was a scientific genius, but did he know as much about poetry as he did about physics? Tiger Woods knew more about golf by the time he was 15 than most adults ever will, but is he just as knowledgeable about general accounting?

What about you? Do you know just the right amount about everything worth knowing? Did you retain everything you were taught as a child? Did your school cover all the right subjects?

While we're at it, what *are* the right subjects? Many have tried to make that determination but cannot come to any kind of permanent agreement. Our federal government has often set standards that dictate what children should know in order to graduate from public education, and those standards have been changed by different administrations. Remember Goals 2000? Or how about the No Child Left Behind (NCLB) program? Each election cycle brings a new program of standards, it seems.

Who Determines the Bases?

Once special interest groups get involved, more confusion develops. For example, most experts agree that history is an important subject, but whose history, and from whose viewpoint? Should it include any religious interpretation, and if so, which religions should be represented? Which should be excluded? You see how complicated a determination of the right subject can get. Now multiply that by all the possible subjects, and you can see that establishing One Body of Knowledge is an impossible task.

Individual schools don't even agree on what should be taught and when it should be taught. When I was a child, my family moved a few times during my grammar school years, and as a result I never learned about liquid measures. Each school I attended had either covered it earlier or intended to teach it later, so I never learned about it until I was forced to, once I started cooking.

Cultures also differ in what is considered essential knowledge. Some Eastern European countries place a greater emphasis on math and science than America does. My husband has worked with Eastern European immigrants, and he says their mathematical abilities far exceed those of average Americans.

Past generations have also had different ideas of what children should be taught. Our grandparents considered beautiful penmanship one essential goal of American education. If you have inherited any letters or documents from your ancestors, you can't help but notice how perfect their handwriting was. But for our computer-dependent times, perfect penmanship is no longer essential. As long as you know how to sign your name, being able to type will get you the rest of the way.

My generation was taught to use the slide rule. Now calculators and computers have erased the need for it. Many schools have eliminated the teaching of sewing because of the wide availability and affordability of ready-made clothes. The changing times also change the value of certain types of knowledge.

The Scope and Sequence

Despite the ever-changing amount and quality of knowledge in our world, many organizations and institutions establish their own versions of One Body of Knowledge. Public and private schools generally use a Scope and Sequence to plan their school year. This is a document that results from a committee's decisions about what children should learn and when they should learn it. It lists all the subjects to be taught in each grade.

Many homeschoolers find a Scope and Sequence valuable, as it gives them a framework and a timetable, which can be comforting. But they should keep in mind that a traditional Scope and Sequence is arranged in cyclical fashion. It keeps coming back to each subject each year, adding a little more information each time while reviewing what was taught in previous years. This is so that the children who didn't pick up much the first time get additional opportunities to do so in subsequent grades. Those who did pick it up the first time, however, must content themselves with receiving small bites of the subject each year, and repetitive reviews that they don't need. That can pretty much kill any interest they might have had in the subject at the beginning.

A child's curiosity doesn't follow a Scope and Sequence. Once he's discovered something interesting, he wants to learn more about it right then, not a year later. Providing him with books and resources related to the subject will allow him to learn until he is sated in that particular area. Child-driven learning has much more staying power than learning about a given subject at a certain time just because it's on the Scope and Sequence for that year.

A Scope and Sequence is set up for the convenience of the classroom teacher, who must try to aim for the middle of the wide array of abilities that each group of students possesses. That is one of the greatest disadvantages of group schooling, and something the homeschooling parent doesn't have to worry about, thanks to the opportunity for one-on-one teaching that homeschooling provides. Nevertheless, some homeschooling parents prefer to use a Scope and Sequence as a framework for their homeschooling.

Obtaining a Scope and Sequence

There are many ways to obtain a Scope and Sequence. You can:

• request one from your local school district
• obtain one from a homeschool curriculum company (A Beka provides a detailed Scope and Sequence on its Web site:

http://www.abeka.com/Resources/PDFs/ScopeAndSequence.pdf)

    • obtain one from an encyclopedia company; some hand these out when exhibiting their products at homeschool conventions

    • do an Internet search using the phrases "Scope And Sequence" or "Lesson Plans"; one large site full of lesson plans is www.lessonplanspage.com. Some states have replaced the phrase "Scope and Sequence" with "Standards of Learning"; an Internet search using that phrase and your state's name will tell you if your state uses "Standards of Learning"

    Other versions of One Body of Knowledge can be found in the many books published over the past few decades that list recommendations for what a child should learn at each grade level. One specific example is the series of books written by E.D. Hirsch, Jr. entitled *What Your "Nth" Grader Needs to Know*. You can buy a related Scope and Sequence by going to www.coreknowledge.org.

    Books like those in Hirsch's series are useful if you need help deciding what to cover. They are generally divided by subject, and contain many ideas and book lists for your use. Of course, in any of these books, the determination of which subjects to cover and how to cover each is merely the opinion of the author combined with his or her research. You may agree with all of it, some of it, or none of it. But if you are mostly in agreement, this type of book could provide you with a foundation to work from, which may make you feel more secure.

    If you choose to base your child's home education on a framework culled from this type of book, try not to look at the author's suggestions as requirements. The pressure you and your child would be under to cover every single recommendation in the book would surely result in burnout. Instead, set priorities by considering which recommendations you deem most important, and which would be of the most interest to your child.

Using a Packaged Curriculum

If you use a packaged curriculum with your child, the designers of the curriculum most likely referred to a Scope and Sequence. The catalogs of companies selling packaged curriculum will usually include a chart of the subjects covered at each grade level, and you can use that as a general indication of what's being done in that grade.

Parents who prefer to use packaged curriculum to homeschool their children can generally assume that the bases being covered are at least on the same level as those in the public schools, and quite possibly on a higher level. Many of the large-scale homeschool curriculum suppliers started out as private school suppliers, so they already had a Scope and Sequence in place before venturing into the homeschool market. Most private schools are more scholastically challenging than public schools; the curriculum they use will be more advanced, too.

Designing Your Own Curriculum

Parents using packaged curriculum can rest assured that their children are being exposed to the same subjects as those in formal school. But what about the parents who prefer a more eclectic, child-led approach? How can they design a plan that will cover all the appropriate subjects?

The answer to this question depends on how the parent defines appropriate. Some parents may feel that an emphasis on reading classic literature is extremely important, but only basic math is needed. Other parents may think that as long as a child learns to read, it doesn't matter what kind of books the child eventually does read. They'd prefer to put their energies into teaching math and science because they believe their child needs to be prepared for a world of rapidly changing technology.

In homeschooling, there are as many educational preferences as there are parents. So does that mean some parents are on the right track and some are on the wrong one? So-called educational experts would say that anyone not following a Scope and Sequence designed by other educational experts is on the wrong track. But the beauty of homeschooling is that the parent is the expert on the child. No one knows that child better than Mom and Dad.

What Should Your Children Learn?

So the ball is in your court. What do you think your child should learn? It can be illuminating to sit down and make a list of:

• what you learned in school that was useful or important to you

• what you wish you would have learned in school but didn't

• what today's publicly-schooled students aren't learning that you want your children to learn

• what your goals are for your children (i.e. self-sufficiency, college prep, technical know-how)

•what your children want to learn

Using Your Own Experience

First, what did you learn in school that helped you? Most adults can agree that learning to read, write and do math are all useful pursuits with long-lasting rewards. Those should go at the top of the list. What else? Try to remember your favorite classes. Chances are you liked them because you enjoyed the subject matter.

Next, think about what you wish you had learned in school. Perhaps you were taught to read in a school using the Whole Language method, and as a result, you still have trouble pronouncing unfamiliar words. Sounds like you'll want to include phonics in your plans for your children. I remember all the struggles I had with something they called the New Math. For that reason, I used a very traditional math program with my children.

Looking at Today's Children

Once you've dug up as many memories as you can, fast forward to the present. Anyone who reads a newspaper or listens to the news is aware that many people are unhappy with public education in our country. Some children aren't learning very much. This results in sad tales of high school students who can't read beyond a third-grade level, and other travesties.

Then there are the publicly schooled children you know personally. Have you noticed holes in their areas of knowledge? When I taught a fourth-grade Sunday school class for several years, I was frequently surprised by the differences in what the students knew because they came from various nearby towns, and therefore different schools.

For example, some were clueless about even the most basic recent history, and others were well-versed in current events. The difference in reading and spelling ability was quite noticeable. Some of the students wrote in cursive, while others preferred drawing pictures because they struggled so much with printing.

Needless to say, my observations of those students' abilities (or lack thereof) affected my decision-making when I planned out my own children's school year. Have you noticed certain things lacking in the education of your young relatives or neighbors? Which things bother you the most? You'll want to make sure your own children aren't lacking in those areas.

What Are Your Goals for Your Children?

Next, what are your goals for your children? Do you hope that all of them will go to college? Is it very important to you that they become computer-literate? Do you insist on plenty of exposure to culture, to music, to art? Is it important to you that they learn all about their government and how to be responsible citizens? What about practical skills, like cooking and repairing things?

We all have different ideas of what is important to know about and experience in life. You and your spouse should discuss what you each want your children to know, and what your goals are for each of your children. These should figure heavily in what you decide to teach them. Since it's impossible to cover everything, set some priorities that will guide you.

What Do Your Children Want to Learn?

Finally, what do your children want to learn? This question is extremely important. Hopefully, it's one of the main reasons you're homeschooling—so that your children can learn about things in which they're interested. As stated earlier, child-driven learning has much more staying power than learning about a given subject at a certain time just because it's on a Scope and Sequence.

So, how do you determine what they want to learn? One way is to be observant. You're probably already aware of some of their areas of interest. You can tell just by the types of questions each one asks. Their habits are another clue. The child who can spend hours making things with building toys will be fascinated by learning how things work. The one who read board books in the crib likely will be eager to read good literature later on.

Another way to determine what your children want to learn is to brainstorm. Sit down with them and ask them what they'd like to learn this year. Write down every idea they come up with, no matter how unrelated all the different ideas may be. It's amazing to hear all the things they're curious about, and the more they talk, the more enthused they get.

Some of the topics will be related. You may hear a lot of science-related topics, for example. This gives you some direction. You can start watching for science project ideas, science books, science curriculum and science-related field trips.

Suppose they mention historical topics that they want to learn about. When my older children wanted to learn about ancient Rome, we bought and borrowed books about the ancient Romans, and made a model of a Roman city. Years later, when my younger daughter expressed an interest in ancient Egypt, I found a hieroglyphics kit for her, and she enjoyed learning about how the ancient Egyptians communicated by writing.

A Customized Scope and Sequence

Once you've determined some answers to the question of what your children should learn, you can design your own customized Scope and Sequence. First, set some priorities for the coming year. Emphasize areas that *both* you and your children want to cover, because you'll be more enthusiastic about finding materials and they'll be more enthusiastic about using those materials.

Don't be afraid to combine areas. For instance, if you want an emphasis on art and they want to learn more about our country's beginnings, use your imagination to come up with ways to do both. Obtain art books from the public library that include paintings of George Washington, the ride of Paul Revere, and the signing of the Declaration of Independence. The children can sketch or paint copies of a few of those works of art. Now go further. Find some good children's stories about the Revolutionary War that can be read aloud or individually. You just added Literature. If any of the stories mention something the characters ate, hunt up the recipe (the Internet is good for this) and let the children try making it. Now you've mixed in Home Economics.

This type of approach is called Unit Studies, and it will help you cover many different subjects on your personalized Scope and Sequence.

The State and Your Customized Scope and Sequence

You could make a fine Customized Scope and Sequence just by combining your goals for your children and their interests. But you also have to include the requirements of the state in which you live.

If these overlap, as they likely will in some areas, no problem. But if the state requires a subject neither you nor your children care to study much, you will have to find a way to satisfy the state while making the subject palatable to you and your children. Try studying homeschool catalogs and product reviews in homeschool magazines to find a game, book or curriculum that will cover that subject. Ask homeschooling friends for their recommendations. Check out homeschool Web sites on the Internet. Look into educational software. With the growing abundance of homeschool materials on the market these days, you should be able to find something that will satisfy the state and your family.

How Much Time Should Be Spent On Each Subject?

Some states require you to cover a subject for a certain number of hours per year. But many do not, and if you are one of the fortunate residents of those states, you now find yourself wondering how much is enough? Take math, for example. Should your children study math every day? Every other day? Once a week?

If your state does not specify a frequency, the decision is up to you. Most homeschooling parents were formally schooled, so we're used to looking at schooling in terms of class periods and semesters. But those concepts were designed for the convenience of the school system. They really have nothing to do with children and how they learn.

Think back to when your children were babies learning to crawl. Did you set aside 30 minutes after lunch for crawling class? Of course not. There were times when your babies wriggled and squirmed and tried to launch themselves forward, and just as many times when they lay on the floor chewing on a toy and watched the world go by. Over time, the wriggling and squirming times increased, though at various times of the day (and night, unfortunately for you). Then one day you found your little one behind the sofa, pleased as punch to have gotten there on his or her own. Soon crawling became second nature.

This is how children learn. Their curiosity drives them until they've learned what they wanted to know. Once they're sated, they move on to something new. If their natural curiosity is not snuffed out by formal education, they will continue to learn that way as they grow older.

So don't be afraid to give them some autonomy when it comes to determining how long to study a subject. Provide books, resources and time. If allowed to learn about something on their own timetable, children will usually stop when they're satisfied. For example, one of your children may develop an interest in Renaissance Art. But after reading books about Renaissance Art, repeatedly playing a Renaissance Art game, recreating Renaissance Art using art supplies, and visiting every museum that contains an example of Renaissance Art within a 50-mile radius, your child decides that's enough of Renaissance Art. By then, you may also feel that the topic has been covered well enough, and doesn't need to be repeated next year (or possibly ever).

One more thing about stopping when your child has reached the saturation point on a given subject: there's nothing wrong with leaving a book unfinished. "We have to keep doing this because we're not done with the book yet" has more to do with "doing school" than with educating a child. It's OK to stop using a book or curriculum when it's not working anymore, or when your child has moved on to a new interest.

But What If They Don't Want to Learn About _____ (fill in the blank)?

There may be some subjects in which your child has no interest, or perhaps he or she delves a little ways into a subject and then loses interest. Does that mean the end of studying that subject?

That depends on you. If your child's curiosity about math was sated by third grade, you may want to assign math at some point later on. It will be hard to function in the world with no math knowledge beyond simple multiplication. On the other hand, you can be patient and wait until your child starts needing math to answer questions in his or her own life (see "Watching for Signs of Readiness" on page 87 for more about math). For example, if your child is saving up for a new toy, and wants to know how many weeks' worth of allowance it will cost, math will suddenly become necessary.

Your comfort level is important here. If you can wait until natural curiosity turns up, fine. If it will drive you up the wall to have an 11-year-old who can't divide yet, better include regular math lessons.

Which Subjects Are the Most Important?

Which are the most important subjects? If your state doesn't require you to follow its take on that, you need to make that decision. So let's cut to the chase. What do you think your child should know?

Everyone can agree on the importance of the "three R's": Reading, Writing and Arithmetic. A young person who can read and comprehend the written word, communicate in writing, and use and understand numbers has a very basic education. These days, the public schools can't even guarantee that. But most homeschooling parents want their children to have more than just a basic education.

How far to go in each of these areas is another consideration, something that is primarily answered by each child's abilities. For some children, reading becomes second nature very quickly, and achieving a high reading level early on is likely. For others, reading will be a struggle, and reading success will be modest and hard-earned.

Writing is similar, in that while competent writing can be learned, true writing ability is a talent that can be nurtured, but not manufactured. If you desire to help each of your children to be the best they can be, your provision of good reading materials and the time to enjoy them will help your children's reading and writing levels come out where they should be.

Arithmetic is a subject on which many homeschooling parents disagree. Some believe their children should eventually master calculus, while others will be satisfied if their children can balance a checkbook and understand compound interest. How much math is enough should be determined by the parents, who are most familiar with each child's abilities, interests and goals.

Beyond the Basics

What about history, science, religion, and music? Then there are practical subjects such as cooking, sewing and crafts. Which should be included, and which should be left out?

Each homeschooling family's choice of subjects will vary, and rightly so. Any given child will like different subjects at different ages. Work toward exposure to many subjects, and specialization in a few. We've already discussed brainstorming to determine your children's interests, but don't be afraid to add new things, too. A simple project or a new book about an unfamiliar subject could spark a lifelong interest. If you see something intriguing at a homeschool convention exhibit hall, buy it. Flipping through a homeschool catalog can also reveal things your children might enjoy.

Remember, you don't have to choose all the subjects ahead of time. The interests of your children will change as they grow, and will provide you with subjects to cover.

Is Timing Really Everything?

There are many different theories on when a child should learn something. Take musical instruments, for example. Our four-year-old neighbor is learning to play a violin using the Suzuki method. My own daughter didn't start playing the violin until age 11. John Holt began playing the cello as an adult.

Some Suzuki proponents insist preschool is the best time to start playing. We waited until our daughter asked to play an instrument. John Holt didn't start until he was well into adulthood. Who's right?

You can always find someone to tell you that you should've started your child on something earlier than you did, and someone else to tell you that you started too soon. Parental experts are everywhere, including those who have no children of their own. But you're the expert when it comes to your children. You need to trust your judgment of what the best time is for each of your children to learn or do something.

Some "experts" will tell you that if you don't take the window of opportunity that a certain chronological age provides, you will miss out on giving your child the best chance to learn something. For example, there are some who believe that a child can only learn to read well if instruction in "pre-reading skills" is begun at age 3 (or 4, or 2, depending on the "expert"). Yet there are homeschooled children who were not instructed in reading at all. Their parents merely answered their questions ("What's this word, Mom?") and provided them with plenty of reading material. They taught themselves to read without ever having been taught "pre-reading skills." They learned to read when they were ready.

Watching for Signs of Readiness

Dr. Raymond and Dorothy Moore, in their book *The Successful Homeschool Family Handbook*, described some homeschooled children whose parents waited for signs of readiness. As a result, these children did not read until age 11 or 12. 12! Does that scare you? And yet, within a few years, they were reading at an adult level. What does that tell you about the many years professional educators assume it takes for children to learn to read?

Then there's math. In *Free at Last; The Sudbury Valley School*, Daniel Greenberg relates the story of a dozen 9–12-year-olds at the school who decided they wanted to learn arithmetic. Since the school was set up to be a place where children learn on their own timetable, these children had never been taught arithmetic because they had not expressed any interest in learning about it up until then. So Greenberg found an 1898 math primer that included plenty of exercises for self-study, and set up arithmetic classes twice a week for as long as it took the children to learn basic math. Each class lasted 30 minutes, and then the children were sent off with exercises to do on their own time, which they would hand in at the next class.

Once the children had mastered addition, subtraction, multiplication (including memorization of the multiplication tables), division, fractions, decimals, percentages and square roots, Greenberg tallied up the total classroom hours. The total was 20 hours.

Somewhat shocked, Greenberg consulted a public school math specialist who told him that twenty hours was about right for interested students, because math really isn't that difficult. He said teaching math took six years or more in the public schools because the students were unwilling and disinterested, and so it had to be fed to them in small doses over a long time.

What If We Leave Something Out?

Some homeschooling parents fear that without an "official" Scope and Sequence to follow, they might leave out something important. They worry that someday, their children's education will have holes in it, because they, the parents, failed to "cover all the bases".

As stated at the beginning, no one learns everything. It just isn't possible to learn everything there is to know, not by the time a person is 18, and not by the time they die of old age. So what to include and what to leave out is a total judgment call.

Parents should also remember that they will not be the sole source of education for their children. One of the greatest gifts you can give your children is the opportunity to educate themselves. Once they know where to look for information, and if their natural curiosity hasn't been snuffed out by formal schooling, the sky is the limit in terms of their education.

Achievement Testing

Some states require homeschooled children to take achievement tests, but many do not. Just because your state doesn't require you to test your children is no reason to avoid doing it on your own. While there's no question that testing has its flaws, testing provides some benefits for homeschoolers, and one of them is reassurance.

If you've been homeschooling for a few years, and you really don't have any idea if your children are making progress compared to children in formal schools, go ahead and test them. I did that with my oldest two children when they were around 7 and 8. Their scores came back anywhere from two to six grade levels above average. That did wonders for my self-confidence, and you can bet I let the relatives know about it, too. We got very few skeptical questions about homeschooling from them after that.

I was so thrilled with the results of that testing episode that I signed my children up for testing the following year. However, as I mentioned earlier, we did no homeschooling in the three months prior to the test date, due to a medical crisis in our family. Yet both children's test scores showed they had gone up an average of two grade levels since the previous test. That helped me realize that my kids were learning on their own, even without my instruction.

If your state requires testing, be aware that most schools spend a great deal of time teaching to the test. In my state, public school children spend about a month before the test date just preparing for the annual state achievement test. So their scores will be somewhat inflated due to that preparation. Keep that in mind when you compare your children's scores to the average.

Another benefit of testing is that it will show if there are any subjects to which a student needs more exposure. The first time my son took the ACT, his scores reflected similar percentiles for every subject except reading comprehension, which lagged a bit behind the others. So I bought a high school level book that included exercises to improve reading comprehension, and my son worked with it twice a week. The following year his reading score went up five points, which really brought up his composite score. Since ACT scores affect not only college admission but scholarship awards, we consider that effort time and money well-spent.

Homeschooling parents who test their children using achievement tests have helped researchers learn more about the many positives of homeschooling. For example, studies of achievement test results of homeschoolers in recent years have shown that:

• homeschoolers generally score 15–30% higher than their publicly schooled peers in the same grade. Since about 25% of homeschoolers study at a level one or more grades higher than their publicly schooled peers, that 15–30% figure is conservative.
• homeschoolers score on average above the 80th percentile in all subjects (the national average is 50%)
• homeschoolers generally have lower problem behavior scores, more positive self-concepts and are less peer-dependent
• homeschooled children of parents who are certified teachers do no better than other homeschooled children
• Canadian homeschoolers score just as high as American homeschoolers

You can research similar studies on the Internet, and learn more about obtaining achievement testing for your children. Useful Web sites include:

www.nheri.org (Web site of the National Home Education Research Institute)

www.hslda.org (Web site of the Home School Legal Defense Association)

http://www.bjupress.com/services/testing (Web site of Bob Jones University Press, which offers the Iowa Test of Basic Skills and the Stanford Achievement Test)

www.baysideschoolservices.com (Web site of Bayside School Services, which offers achievement testing that homeschooling parents can use with their children at any time of the year)

www.thurbers.net (Web site of Thurber's Educational Assessments, which offers the California Achievement Test for grades K–12)

Don't be intimidated by testing, especially if you're going to test your children on your own to satisfy your curiosity about how they'll do. Treat it as something fun and different, and try not to make a big deal out of it. It makes a nice change of pace for a few days, and the only preparation your children really need is to be able to follow directions and fill in those little ovals on the scannable sheet. If you think they need more preparation than that, you can use the practice tests that come with the test, or buy an age-appropriate test preparation book. McGraw Hill publishes a line called Spectrum Test Prep for grades K–8 that includes practice tests in many different subjects. Rainbow Resource Center (www.rainbowresource.com) sells these books, and I have also seen them at Borders bookstores.

If you think testing would be of help to your homeschool efforts, but don't want to do it alone, you can organize a testing session among the homeschoolers you know. One mom I know did this by hiring a test administrator and using a local church's facility. It was set up co-op style, with the parents of participating children helping in the testing rooms as proctors, in the nursery caring for the infants of the other helping parents, and supervising children playing outside between testing periods.

Testing should be spread over two to three days, as it takes up to six hours total, and the children need some breaks between tests. Test results are confidential, and sent directly to the parents. Most tests cost between $25–50 per child, plus the shared cost of the test administrator, if the testing service requires one. Test administrators are usually other homeschooling parents who hold bachelor's degrees and have been specially trained by the test provider. Some homeschooling parents work as test administrators to provide extra income for their families.

One caution: some children become very anxious about testing and don't perform well, while some others can "read" the intentions of the test writer and make really good guesses at the questions they don't know. Either of these situations will skew those children's test scores to some extent. Don't put all your faith in test scores, but use them as a general guide, and most likely, as an encouragement to you that your children are doing just fine.

A Final Bit of Encouragement

The fact that you're worried about "covering all the bases" shows that you're a concerned, conscientious parent who wants the best for each of your children. Since you've got the concerned part down pat, let's look at the logical side of things.

You know your children better than any so-called expert. You raised them, you know their strengths and their weaknesses, and you can tell when they're interested in something and when they're merely going through the motions. They can't pull the wool over your eyes. This knowledge equips you to be their best teacher, and should empower you and give you confidence.

No so-called expert, no high-falutin' education professional and no bureaucrat can tell you how to educate your children. You need to take your knowledge of your children and consider it your Ph.D. in education. Be willing to make the decisions about what they should learn through homeschooling. Be ready to listen and act on their expressed desires of what they want to learn. You can't pour knowledge into their heads, but you can facilitate their ability to learn.

While you're at it, take a look around you. Homeschooling works! Kids who were homeschooled by all different methods are winning bees and contests. Homeschooled teenagers are being recruited by colleges, and many are already running successful businesses. Their numbers are increasing. Behind every one of them are homeschooling parents who were just like you once, wondering if they were doing enough of the right things. They were, as it turns out, and you will, too.

OVERCOMING OBSTACLES TO HOMESCHOOLING

You will be confronted by obstacles in almost anything you undertake in life; homeschooling is certainly no exception to that rule. Although parents from around the world are successfully homeschooling their children, none of them find it to be smooth sailing all of the time. They've just learned to overcome the obstacles. If you're prepared for the obstacles you may face, you'll be ready to handle them and move on.

Parents might expect that their children would present most of homeschooling's obstacles because of misbehavior, reluctance to work, etc., but I've found that most obstacles come from other sources. What they are and how to handle them can be found in this section.

The success of our homeschooling effort largely depends on the homeschooling parent (let's say homeschooling mom, since more moms than dads actually do the homeschooling) to get it off the ground and keep it there.

Since homeschooling is a relatively new phenomenon in our culture, the overwhelming majority of us did not know we would eventually do this. That explains why so many of the habits we had in our pre-homeschooling lives can actually work against us now, as we pursue a homeschooling lifestyle. In fact, such habits are often obstacles to our success as homeschooling moms. Just as we had to change some habits when we became parents (for example, late nights with friends became late nights with the baby), there are habits we need to break once we become homeschoolers.

There are also certain aspects of our personalities that can make homeschooling harder than it has to be. If we can recognize them, we can effect changes in our thoughts and ways of doing things that will help instead of hinder our homeschooling efforts.

Finally, at times we may find ourselves in circumstances that make homeschooling difficult. How we deal with those circumstances can make the difference between success or failure at homeschooling.

The commodity homeschooling moms need most is time. It seems as though there aren't enough hours in the day to keep up with the house, the meals, the shopping, and the million other things in a mom's job description, much less homeschooling. Overcoming these obstacles will give us more time to do what we need to do.

PERSONAL HABITS

We pick up different habits during youth, single adulthood and marriage (before children). Some are bad habits, others harmless, but we now find that some of them are holding us back as we homeschool. They may be so ingrained that we don't realize the trouble they are creating for us. Some of these may not apply to you, but others may nag at your conscience. Here are some of the most common:

Television

The boob tube, the idiot box, the squawker . . . the television has a lot of nicknames, none of them flattering. So many people are critical of television, and claim not to watch it much, but if that's the case, how do we explain the millions of people paying $50 each month for cable television or satellite dish usage? Let's face it, today's parents were raised on television, and we've been watching it since we were tiny. It is one very difficult habit to break.

It has its advantages, of course. When you're tired, you can crash in front of it and relax. Sometimes, there's actually something worthwhile on. And if it weren't for television, how could we watch our favorite movies?

But it has big disadvantages. Stay-at-home moms who miss hearing adult conversation may use it for company, and end up wasting large chunks of time. Meanwhile, their children are left to their own devices. If school work is being postponed until Mom's show is over, that sets a really bad example for the children.

If you have a problem getting away from the television, you need to break that habit. You'll be shocked at how much more free time you have, and if there's one thing all homeschool moms need more of, it's time. Whether you go cold turkey and stop all television viewing, or put yourself on a TV diet of just the news, or only your favorite sitcom, limiting your TV time will free you up to do the things you know you should be doing instead.

Internet

Like television, the Internet is one of those distractions that can eat up lots of time with little payback. On the other hand, the Internet provides useful information, and keeps us in touch with friends and loved ones. So the Internet is a good thing, right?

It depends. How much time are you spending online? If you find yourself surfing or chatting idly for hours, think about all the other things you could have accomplished during that time. I have struggled with this issue on and off for years. I find that if I listen to my conscience, I know when I'm doing something worthwhile (researching an upcoming purchase, keeping up with current events, staying in touch with people I care about) and when I'm wasting time (passing on silly forwards, "googling" former classmates, over-researching any subject). Others I know spend a large amount of time "chatting" online.

Most of the chatter is a waste of time, the homeschooler's most precious commodity.

If you're Internet-addicted, try keeping a timer nearby and setting it for 30 minutes. You can get a lot accomplished when you're "on the clock," and you probably won't spend your limited time surfing aimlessly. Once the timer rings, log off before you can rationalize another 30 minutes.

Telephone

Speaking of useless chatter, the telephone can be a major time-waster, and women particularly seem to succumb to it.

We've all seen them wandering through the grocery, chattering away on their cell phones, oblivious to their surroundings. These conversations rarely sound necessary ("Hi, whatcha doin'?" does not suggest urgency), and often consist primarily of gossip. Where women used to be able to spend hours on the phone in the privacy of their homes (my mother was one of those), now they are on display for everyone to see, in stores, cars and even public bathrooms (yuck!). The advent of cordless and cellular phones made this habit more apparent to the rest of the world, because now the yakkers are not anchored to the kitchen wall or the hall desk as they once were.

As busy as they are, homeschoolers cannot afford to waste hours on the phone. But homeschooling can sometimes be lonely, because even though you're surrounded by little people, you still need some adult conversation. The way to deal with this is to keep your phone conversations reasonably short, and save those marathon sessions for personal visits and homeschool support group events.

For homeschoolers, the biggest problem with spending the day with the phone in your ear is that it deprives your children of your attention. When your child has a question, his curiosity is piqued now. It may have disappeared by the time you get off the phone with Aunt Ida an hour from now.

This is not to say that your children should feel like they can interrupt you whenever they want. But if you tend to spend a lot of time on the phone, they feel like they never get a chance to talk to you. They have to interrupt you if you're perpetually taking and making calls. Try relying on an answering machine or voice mail when you're working with your children. The rest of the time, limit the length and the quantity of your calls. Then it will be easier to train your children not to interrupt you, because they know they'll get their chance shortly.

Shopping

This is a tough one for homeschooling moms, because the nature of our work requires that we find and buy lots of supplies for our families: food, clothing, household needs, furniture, and of course, books, curriculum and school supplies. Obviously, shopping is a large part of our lives out of necessity.

The problem arises when the shopping takes over our lives, and causes us to spend too much time and money. This can be an especially difficult problem for the homeschool mom who was a shopaholic before she had children. Perhaps shopping was one of your hobbies when you were younger, and you spent hours in malls looking for just the right blouse. Maybe shopping was your favorite way of passing time, even if you weren't look- ing for anything in particular. This could be a real problem for you, because you don't have that kind of time anymore, yet you are responsible for the large amount of purchasing your family requires.

To break this habit, limit the amount of time you spend shopping and the number of stores you go to. Homeschooling doesn't leave enough time for you to hit a different store each day. Keep a running list at home of what you need, and when the time comes that something is needed urgently, go out and buy it and as many other things on your list as you can find. Then avoid stores until the next urgent need arises. In a family, that will happen soon enough.

Shopaholics often tend to buy too much, especially when it comes to sale items. Keep in mind that if you overbuy clothes, toys, and curriculum, you will soon be tripping over the excess when it's outgrown. Try to buy just what you need instead of more than you need.

Exercise

We know exercise is good for us, but you can have too much of a good thing. There's a difference between a need and an addiction, and some women find themselves addicted to exercise. After having a few babies, they see what's happened to their bodies, and they panic. The next thing they know, their lives revolve around their gym visits.

If you're fitting your homeschooling in around your exercise schedule, something needs to change. Instead of leaving your children out of the exercise equation, include them. Try to incorporate bike rides, nature walks and competitive games in your homeschool. Of course, you'll call it P.E. This provides you and your children with much-needed exercise, and you'll save a lot of money on that gym membership, too.

PERSONALITY-DRIVEN OBSTACLES

A habit can be broken, but your personality can't be changed. You can, however, become aware of certain aspects of your personality that are holding you back, and train yourself to control them.

Since a successful homeschooling experience results from a combination of child-led learning and mom-led organizing, your personality figures largely in your success as a homeschooler. Your strengths will help your homeschooling effort, and your weaknesses can hurt it. Becoming aware of certain personality deficits can lead you to control them, and results in an easier homeschooling experience.

A few specific personality traits stand out as being especially difficult to deal with when homeschooling. Over the years, I have struggled with some of these, as have many of my homeschooling friends. These traits are hard to shake, but becoming aware of them is the first step toward dealing with them. They include:

The Constant Motion Personality

She wants to be going places and doing things all the time, so that she and her children don't miss out on anything. Her vehicle is her most vital possession, and it is strewn with food, toys, clothes and many other necessities of life on the road. There is no class she won't sign her children up for, and no field trip she can miss, because she can never say no to an activity.

If this sounds familiar, consider that in order to homeschool, you need to be home sometimes. And if your homelife is chaotic, with mess everywhere and no food in the house, accept the fact that you can't catch up unless you stay home more than occasionally.

When it comes to activities and field trips, think about this: if your children go to homeschool co-op two days a week, attend homeschool sports one day a week, and go on one field trip or park day per week, they are spending about as much time in organized school as the kids in public school, once you subtract all those teacher in-service days. It's not homeschooling if you're never home.

Homeschooled children are blessed with time in their daily lives to explore their own interests. I see many of our friends' and neighbors' children who are completely booked, day and night, with organized activities, and I feel so sorry for them.

It wasn't like that when I was young. We had little homework, and spent our hours away from school doing what we wanted to do. Outside of chores, my time was my own. But many of today's parents (even some homeschooling parents) are caught up in an unspoken competition to determine whose child is the busiest.

My husband and I limited our children's organized activities so that they had free time every day. When you think about it, there are really only two times in your life that you get much free time: during childhood and during retirement. In between those two lie years and years of work and responsibility for other people. Why would we want to cheat our children of their early years of freedom?

I don't have a problem with organized sports, or art classes, or gymnastics, or Scouts. In fact, my children have done all of those things, but not at the same time. That's key; you need to take on activities one at a time, and only sign up your children if they ask you to. If you hear of some activity that you feel you simply must put them in, make sure you're not just transferring your own aspirations to them. Yes, you probably could have been a soccer star if you'd had the opportunity 30 years ago, but that doesn't mean they must be soccer stars now. Unless they show interest in it, skip it.

As for field trips, we don't do them anymore unless it's something that we just can't pass up, because I learned to limit the amount of running around we do. Over the years, I've seen so many homeschooling families wear themselves out going to every field trip they could find, plus sports and dance classes and gymnastics and you-name-it. We have found that it is much more productive to put in lots of "face time" at home, where it's you and your child reading or talking or making something. You can't give your children much face time if all they ever see is the back of your head from the back seat of the van.

The Teacher Personality

She either wanted to be a teacher, or has been one, or just has fond memories of the way she remembers her own early school years. Or maybe she was just a big fan of "Romper Room." Regardless, the teacher personality tries to recreate her ideal of school by replicating it in her home. She puts in long hours making detailed lesson plans, turns the basement into a "school room" complete with desks and globe, and divides her children's day into inviolable class periods.

The problem here is that once the novelty wears off, the children tire of this, and lose all their enthusiasm for learning. The school atmosphere was designed to handle many children at one time. The detailed lesson plans leave no room for spontaneity or children's many questions. The rows of desks are meant to keep a crowd in line, not a family. Dividing the day into periods (and only allowing one specific subject per period) squelches a child's natural curiosity. By establishing such a school in your home, you are effectively extinguishing most of the benefits of homeschooling in favor of the negatives of formal school.

Some people do this automatically, because it means "school," instead of thinking about why formal schools do it that way, which is because of the logistics of handling a crowd. Such limitations are counter-productive in the superior environment of homeschooling. We have the benefits of one-on-one learning, of spontaneity, and of a loving, permanent relationship between the teacher and each of her students, on whom she is an expert. Why settle for anything less?

The teacher personality needs to learn to relax, and to trust her children and herself to take on homeschooling without the shackles. If this sounds like you, start by loosening up on subjects like art, music, and science, and slowly work your way up to the biggies, reading and math. As your children regain their natural enthusiasm, you'll find homeschooling to be much easier than just schooling was.

The Perfectionist Personality

The perfectionist can make homeschooling very difficult because she has such high expectations of herself as well as her children. As many jobs as the homeschool mom has (teacher, mom, cook, chauffeur, etc.), the perfectionist expects to do them all perfectly. That's a lot of pressure to put on yourself.

The mom who's a perfectionist when it comes to her house is in for some frustration. Keeping a pristine house and unblemished furniture is not likely when your children are home every day. Moms with kids in school can vacuum and dust all day if they want to, but homeschooling moms don't have that opportunity. Homeschooling also generates lots of books and projects. At times, learning is just plain messy. The perfectionist homemaker will wear herself out trying to keep a homeschooling house spotless.

If she's a perfectionist about homeschooling, she will find herself on an endless quest to find the perfect curriculum. Sometimes you have to make do with what you can find, and she has a hard time with that concept. She may also expect her children to do all their work perfectly, and that's not fair to them. The learning environment cannot thrive under pressure.

Finally, if she's trying to be the perfect mom, she will be constantly disappointed in herself. Being with your children all the time can be trying, and sometimes moms yell, or overreact, or become overwhelmed. We moms are not invincible, but the mom aiming for perfection thinks that goal is attainable. She'll go through a lot of aspirin trying to get there, and most of the headaches will be self-induced.

Perfectionist moms must let go of their perceived control of everything. They need to allow themselves and their children to make mistakes, because that's how we learn. It's OK if the house doesn't look like Martha Stewart's house. Children don't end up as bums because their handwriting is sloppy or their just-made bed looks lumpy. If you're a perfectionist mom, you and your children will enjoy homeschooling much more if you'll just relax and let everyone (including yourself) be human.

The Low-Confidence Personality

This kind of mom really believes in homeschooling, but worries that she won't do a good enough job of it. Perhaps she feels lacking because she didn't go to college, or if she did go, because she didn't get an education degree.

Does she sound like you? If so, think about the fact that, years ago, young ladies in their late teens (without any college training) often taught in one-room schoolhouses. Before that, many children did not attend school because their parents needed them to work for the family farm or business. Yet two hundred years ago, the U.S. population's literacy rate was 98% (including slaves), and now it's less than 90%. So what have college-trained teachers done for us?

Do you really want to homeschool your children? Motivation is one of the best indicators of a parent who is "qualified" to homeschool. Add to that the fact that the parent knows the child better than anyone else does, and the confidence that develops from that awareness, and you have a very qualified teacher.

So if you are truly motivated to teach your children at home, you've met one requirement. Now think about the abilities your children have already gained under your supervision. You didn't send them to school to teach them to eat, walk, or talk, did you? They learned from your coaching, and your example. So you've already got experience teaching your children. That should give you some confidence in yourself, and confidence is essential.

A Few More Confidence Boosters:
God gave you these specific children, and expects you to do your best with them. He trusts you with their upbringing, so shouldn't you trust yourself? Pray for help when you need it; "Seek and ye shall find."

You've raised your children since birth: who knows them better than you do?

Even a good teacher, when faced with 20 or 30 students, cannot possibly give each one a fraction of the attention you can give your children on a daily basis.

If you need to teach your children about something you know little about, you have the time to sit down with them and learn it together.

You'll have your children during the day, when they are rested and refreshed, and their attention span is the longest. If you send them to school, you'll get what's left of them at the end of the day.

So many studies have shown that, on average, homeschoolers score 15–30% higher than public school students on achievement tests. Do you really think all those homeschoolers' parents have college degrees, much less education degrees?

If you're unsure of yourself, read homeschooling books, talk to other homeschoolers and figure out what boosts your self-confidence when it comes to homeschooling. When your children reach milestones, whether it's learning to read or scoring high on the SAT, pat yourself on the back. Most of all, when you have thoughts that reflect low or no self-confidence, take an appreciative look at your children. You've brought them this far, haven't you?

The Follower Personality

Some homeschooling moms imitate other homeschooling moms. A while back, there was a well-known speaker and writer who was very articulate in describing her large family's lifestyle, which included homeschooling, homesteading in the country, dressing a certain way, growing their own food, home-birthing, etc. She developed a good-sized following among her readers, who wrote to her in increasing numbers about their own efforts to move to the country and live off the land. They questioned her about dress, child-rearing and religion.

But then something happened in her personal life that caused many of her "followers" to realize that she was merely human and fallible, and they responded with letters of anger and grief. Much of their reaction came from the loss of their role model.

You wouldn't expect imitators among homeschoolers, who tend to be an independent bunch, as evidenced by their willingness to buck the system by educating their children at home. But most homeschool moms were educated in formal schools, which promote the role of the follower. Remember the girl in junior high school who was smart, pretty and president of the student council? Many of the other girls wanted to be just like her. Well, now they've grown up, and a few are still looking for role models.

But in many ways, homeschooling is uncharted territory. You don't have to be a homesteading mom, or a hippie mom, or even a famous homeschooler mom. You can be yourself, your best self, because that's what your children deserve. And if there's a mom in your support group who seems to have it all together, you can learn from her without imitating her. Know yourself, and establish a lifestyle and a homeschool that fulfills your children's needs by being yourself. Find books and resources you can work with. Live in a house that fits the way your family lives. By being yourself, you set an example of independence for your children. After all, if you wanted them to learn to be followers, you could have sent them to school.

The Disorganized Personality

For the disorganized, nothing is easy. In order to mail a letter, the stamps must be found, or purchased. In order to make lunch, a quick trip to the grocery must be made. And in order to homeschool, the disorganized mom must shovel off the table, find some pencils, and begin a search for the math book . . . does this sound familiar? If you're a disorganized person, homeschooling will be torture for you; just keeping your family fed and clothed has probably been a challenge.

This must be an issue for many homeschoolers, because there are so many different homeschool organizer notebooks and planners on the market, and they all seem to survive. People are buying them, so there must be a need.

If you buy a system and it works for you, great. While you do need a system that you can live with, the most important thing is to have *some* kind of system. The homeschool mom is the hub of the family, and if she can stay organized, the family will run smoothly. But if she has no system and spends her days putting out fires, very little progress will be made in her family's homeschooling. She will waste that precious learning time trying to find things, keep up with things and finish things.

I've always thought of homeschooling as being like spinning plates. When I was a child, I used to watch performers on television spin plates on the tops of long poles. A performer would start one plate spinning, then several more, and then would run back and forth between poles keeping all the plates spinning atop them. Once in a while, he'd miss one . . . crash!

The homeschool mom runs back and forth between children and the laundry room and the kitchen. She must keep up with her many responsibilities, because a family is a constantly changing organism. Meals are cooked and eaten, and soon it's time for the cycle to repeat. Clothes are washed, dried, folded, put away, worn, dirtied and washed again. The dishwasher runs, is emptied, and quickly refills. The pantry empties and must also be refilled.

Of course, children should help with many of these daily tasks, but Mom must be the overseer who keeps the plates spinning. Without a system, she will run herself ragged.

You'll find many ideas for getting organized in the "On the Home Front" section of this book. Whether you find a system, buy a system, or best of all, design your own system, do something to overcome your tendency toward disorganization. Read books about household organization. Visit Web sites about getting organized. Cull the ideas that you are likely to act on, and start making some changes in your home. Otherwise, homeschooling will become miserable or even impossible.

CIRCUMSTANCES AS OBSTACLES

Sometimes, we find ourselves in circumstances that make homeschooling more difficult than it would be otherwise. Often, these situations are not of our own making, or can't be helped, but they shouldn't keep us from homeschooling if that's what we really want to do. Some are serious, others more annoying or just plain time-consuming, but all of them require us to do some extra thinking about how we can successfully homeschool in the midst of the specific situation.

A Child with Special Needs

We'd been homeschooling for five years when Josh arrived with fuzzy blonde hair, bright blue eyes and Down syndrome. He spent a month in the hospital because of health problems, and then we brought him home, along with his heart/apnea monitor and his medications. In the hospital, we'd been warned that not only should he be put into an early intervention program immediately, but that we wouldn't be able to homeschool him. After we heard about how many therapy visits he'd need, we weren't sure we'd even be able to keep homeschooling his siblings.

As it turned out, we did homeschool all of our children, but only because we made it a priority. We limited our son's therapies to those we considered necessary. During those sessions, his siblings worked on their school assignments in the waiting room. I started reading up on special education, and what I learned led my husband and I to decide that this little guy would benefit from homeschooling at least as much as the others.

There are many families homeschooling children with special needs and their siblings. A wonderful organization, NATHHAN, offers help and hope to them. We've found, as have many other families, that homeschooling brings children and their handicapped sibling closer, because of the time they spend together. In addition, dealing with such a sibling brings out sensitivity in the other children.

Of course, it's not easy. By the time Josh was two, I was having such a hard time keeping up with everything that my husband quit his job and started his own at-home business so that he could help me more. That's probably the only reason we were able to keep homeschooling.

Even now, any plans we make and anywhere we go requires special consideration of our son. He cannot be left unattended, and must be watched outside because he tends to run off. Homeschooling him requires far more "face time" than it did with the others. We can't ever take too much time off because he loses much of what he's been learning.

If you have a child with special needs, don't rule out homeschooling for that child or your others. Talk to homeschoolers who have been there, read "Homeschooling a Child with Special Needs" on page 64 and contact NATHHAN.

Financial Difficulties

Money is tight for many single-income families these days, but if the breadwinner (usually Dad) loses his job, that can be a real emergency. While he searches for a new job, Mom may want to find work to bring in some money. If she starts working, does that mean the end of homeschooling?

Not necessarily. If you are committed to homeschooling, you will want to find ways to bring in money that allow you to keep homeschooling. Some ways others have done this include:

- telecommuting
- in-home daycare
- selling goods via home parties (books, cooking utensils, candles, etc.)
- working retail in the evenings and on weekends
- starting a family business so the kids can help
- delivering newspapers in the wee hours

If none of these options work out, you can always get a day job and let Dad do the homeschooling. He won't do it the same way as you do, but a little change will be good for the kids, and Dad will develop further (or new) appreciation for what you do all day. Once he finds another job, you can quit yours and go back to homeschooling, most likely with renewed vigor.

Whether you're dealing with unemployment or some other kind of financial setback, another option is to cut back drastically on what you spend. A penny saved is not only a penny earned, but a penny earned without paying taxes on it. Until your money situation improves, dedicate yourself and your family to cutting back everywhere you can. Make your children the Utility Police, so that they'll be on the lookout for lights burning in unoccupied rooms, and showers that take too long and waste water. Challenge yourself to see how low you can get that food bill while keeping everyone fed and healthy. Check out some frugal Web sites (www.stretcher.com is a great one) and educate yourself on saving money.

While you're at it, save money on your homeschooling. Use the books and resources you already have instead of buying more just now. If it isn't already your favorite place, make the public library your choice for books, software, and educational videos. Organize a swap meet in your support group so that everyone can try some new things at no cost. Find out if your local museums offer "free days," and if so, visit only on those days.

With some ingenuity and a good attitude, you can get through financial difficulties without giving up homeschooling. Think of what your example will teach your children about perseverance, and what the entire family will learn by working together.

Disapproval of Family and Friends

When someone first learns about homeschooling, and then considers the possibility for her children, enthusiasm begins to develop. The more she reads about homeschooling's advantages, the more excited she gets. Then she brings up the subject around some relatives or friends. Many times, they don't share her excitement. In fact, they may be totally opposed to the idea.

When people you care about are against homeschooling, you have some tough decisions to make. How you make those decisions depends on who's against it.

If your parents, in-laws or other relatives don't like the idea, you have to decide whether their disapproval is something that would stop you from homeschooling. If you have a very close relationship with them, talk to them and find out exactly what worries them. The older generation has a picture in its collective consciousness of school the way it was back in the mid-1900's. Have you ever read the list of teachers' complaints from the early 1960's? It includes such behavior as talking in class and chewing gum. Nowadays, that list includes physical assaults on teachers and gang activities in the schools. But many members of the older generation don't realize that the schools in their areas have such problems. They still picture Miss Smith in her shirtwaist and pearls leading a class in reciting the multiplication tables.

Of course, their memories are tinged in the golden glow of time passed and difficulties forgotten, so they may not understand how you can deny your children the wonderful education they got (or believe they got). Maybe you can calm their fears by citing information you've found, or introducing them to some veteran homeschoolers you know with older homeschooled children. These days, the newspapers are filled with stories of homeschoolers winning spelling and geography bees, and other honors. Clip those stories and pass them on to the naysayers.

Eventually, as they see how well your children are doing, your relatives should relax somewhat. If not, they need to be reminded that you are in charge of your children, and that you are doing what's best for them.

If the dissenters are your children's grandparents, bring them into your homeschooling. Are there subjects they could teach their grandchildren? Perhaps Grandpa is a woodworker, or Grandma loves to play tennis. These are things they could share with your children. The children learn something new, and the grandparents learn that these are smart children you're raising.

As time passes, be sure to keep them up to date on the children's accomplishments. If your children score high on achievement tests, send copies of those test reports as soon as possible. When your support group has a project night, invite the relatives. Let them see for themselves how well homeschoolers are doing.

What about friends and neighbors? They have no clout when it comes to how you raise your children, but it can be difficult to accept that they don't like what you're doing. As for your neighbors, do you realize that by homeschooling your children, you're saying, "I won't put my kids in the school your kids go to, even though I've already paid for it through my taxes." In other words, it's like looking at your neighbor's car or furniture and telling them, "I wouldn't take that if it were free."

So these people may not be all that thrilled with your decision to homeschool. But if you're motivated to homeschool, you'll have to develop a thick skin and continue on your course. You need to do what's right for your family.

Dysfunctional Family

This situation goes beyond disapproving relatives. The dysfunctional family usually includes instances of inappropriate behavior, mental illness or instability, and an unhealthy atmosphere for your children. If any of your relatives fall into this category, you'll have to take care that their problems don't throw you off course in your homeschooling.

Truly dysfunctional families are characterized by strife. There is always some kind of drama going on between its members, complete with angry phone calls, outbursts at family events, and eventually, some members who aren't speaking to other members.

If this doesn't sound like your family, say a prayer of thanks. But for those who come from such a family, and are trying to prevent that kind of situation in their own household, dealing with this issue can become very time-consuming and disruptive.

Your husband and children must come first. This means when you're homeschooling, you cannot stop what you are doing to take a call from your sister, who is mad at your other sister and needs to talk to you about it. Use an answering machine or voice mail if you can't turn her down in real time, but nip this in the bud. In dysfunctional families, squabbles escalate into war very quickly, and you could spend weeks trying to listen to all the sides and settle things.

You also have to be careful not to let the perpetual fighting amongst your relatives affect your mood at home. Your husband and children don't deserve to have you bark at them because you're upset that one of your squabbling relatives insulted you. If these people and their issues start affecting how you deal with your own family, you need to distance yourself from their situations, and if need be, from them.

When you homeschool, keep your mind off the relatives and on what you're doing. When your little girl is reading a story she wrote to you, you should be hearing her, not replaying that last fight with your brother in your head. Kids know when you're really there, and when you're just pretending to give them your attention. The whole point of homeschooling is to give them one-on-one, right?

Finally, try to use the dysfunctional family you came from or married into as an example of what not to do. Don't pit your children against each other. Instead, look for opportunities to teach them to communicate with each other in appropriate ways, and to work together. Don't threaten them with the loss of your love if they make a big mistake someday. Let them know that no matter what happens, you will always be a family and you will always love them. That will provide them with security that will stick with them as they become adults.

Needy Friends

It's important to be a good friend, and it sets a good example for your children when you do so. But sometimes, a friend's needs can collide with your considerable responsibilities as a homeschooling parent, and then what do you do?

This is most likely to happen when you have a needy friend. She's the kind of person who is going through a breakup or a divorce, and needs constant reassurance and comfort. So she calls you to get her through the rough spots. Sometimes, those rough spots occur several times a day. If it's a divorce, she wants to know what you think: should the attorney have done this or that? Should she push for the house, or let him deal with it? What about the judge? Does he sound like a chauvinist to you?

Or maybe she's having trouble with a coworker. Each day during her lunch hour, she calls you in a whisper, describing how the coworker offended her this time. She's looking for a listener as much as for advice, and feels that she must give you every detail in order to make her case.

The problem is, you're not her attorney, and you're not her psychologist. You're a homeschooling mom who is desperately trying to work with her children. They resent the constant interruptions, and when those interruptions take too long, they disappear into their rooms or outside, leaving you stuck on the phone, with no school getting done.

It's hard to turn down a friend who needs your help, but perhaps you're not the one to help. Your needy friend may need professional help, or just the ear of someone who isn't as busy as you are (can't she call her mother about this?) Someday, you will be done homeschooling, and if you want to spend your time dealing with needy friends, you can do so. But for now, you have important work to do, and your children need you.

ONCE THE OBSTACLES ARE GONE

If you recognize some of the obstacles listed here as present in your own life, work to eliminate them one by one. As you overcome them, you will find that your work as a homeschooling mom becomes easier. You'll develop ways of doing things that will streamline your efforts; time for enjoying your family will open up almost magically.

Veteran homeschoolers find that such efforts result in routines and habits that become automatic. Developing efficient ways of doing things and eliminating time-wasters are abilities that will pay off for you not only during your homeschooling years, but after your children are grown. Should you decide to find paid employment once you're done homeschooling, you'll find that employers are looking for employees who know how to get a job done despite obstacles. If you decide to work for yourself, your business will benefit from your ability to deal with difficulties, an ability you developed as a homeschooling mom.

But that's down the road. For now, the most important advantage of overcoming these obstacles is that you'll gain more time for homeschooling: for reading, playing and learning with your children. That's something you and your family can benefit from immediately.

COPING WITH CHANGES AND CHALLENGES

Here are ideas for changing your homeschooling approach, accepting your limitations, homeschooling the child you've just withdrawn from formal school, helping homeschooling friends who have special needs children, and preventing burnout. This section closes with a reminder of what your life would be like if you didn't homeschool.

Changing My Game Plan

Like many people, I began homeschooling by imitating the schools of my youth. I bought a boxful of curriculum, divided it into daily assignments, and taught my kids right out of those books.

And there wasn't anything especially bad about that, except that after the initial excitement wore off, my kids started to get bored. Instead of being excited about doing school, they ranked it right down there with making their beds and setting the table—something we have to do, so let's get it over with.

That was not in my game plan. I didn't want them to be bored. I was bored in school, and I still recalled how bad that felt. I wanted my kids to enjoy school.

What I soon realized was that while they might have been bored with school, my kids still loved learning. They enjoyed visiting museums. My daughter read through stacks of books without my telling her to do so. And my son drew beautiful, detailed pictures that were not assigned by me.

I even became bored by the assignments I was teaching the kids, and it must have been around that time that I came up with the idea of playing store. I labeled some items in our pantry (using prices written on sticky notes), then dug up all the spare change I could find.

119

I became the storekeeper, and the kids became the shoppers. They'd choose an item from the pantry and pay me for it. Often I had to make change for them. Soon they were buying more than one item at a time and figuring out how much they owed me. Before long, they started taking turns being the storekeeper. This became a game they enjoyed for a long time, but I think I probably learned the most from that experience, because I saw that homeschooling didn't have to be boring, like formal school was for me as a child.

This success led me to become more creative with our homeschooling. Since my first two children were only 18 months apart, they studied most subjects together, and that made it easy to come up with math games. Their favorite math game came about by necessity. I was pregnant with our third child, and spending a lot of time on the sofa. While beached there, I'd hold up a flash card, and throw it to whichever child gave the correct answer first. The child who collected the most cards won. Since the kids were very competitive with each other, they soon learned their math facts (which I'd been unsuccessfully trying to force into their heads by using written timed drills, as advised by our curriculum). This way was much easier and a lot more fun.

Making learning fun started to seep into other areas of our homeschooling. I made a little game out of putting the books of the Bible in order. I made small cards with the name of a book on each, and then let the kids put them in order. This way they were using their hands along with their minds, which is always a good way to learn. Soon they could get those cards in order pretty quickly, so they began timing themselves. Naturally, they began comparing their best times, and that led to me making two sets of cards so they could compete directly against each other. Before long, they could quickly find any book of the Bible. And they'd had a lot of fun getting to that point.

Such successes led me to loosen up in our homeschooling, and to be open to using games and other activities. More importantly, I soon came to see those things as at least equal in importance to bookwork. I bought Cuisenaire rods for math, which worked so well that I ended up giving up the formal math curriculum we'd been using, and buying the Miquon Math series instead (you use rods with them). Three of my kids eventually worked through Miquon with the rods, and then went straight into Saxon 54 or 65 with no difficulty.

I also used treasure hunts to teach them, first to follow directions (they were small then so I put pictures on the clues instead of words), and later to read (I switched to clues in short sentences). They begged me to do this all the time. There was no boredom or sighing in this kind of school!

Of course, as they reached their teen years, our use of games decreased, and they had to buckle down to more bookwork. I was concerned that at some point they might have to go to school, and I wanted to keep them at approximate grade level in case that happened. Fortunately, it never did, but by high school, they had regular bookwork and the games had run their course (other than playing educational games like Rummy Roots™ or ElementO®). But while they were younger, we had lots of fun learning through play and games, and I think I learned a lot from seeing that. Maybe that's what it takes to get a formally schooled mom to let go of that old training and accept that learning doesn't have to be boring for kids, and *shouldn't* be boring, either.

It's a good thing I learned that lesson too, because playing games has become the backbone of Josh's homeschooling experience. I've used games to teach him the alphabet, sight words and numbers. He can't just sit and learn easily from formal schoolwork. I've had to get creative when it comes to teaching him: letting go of my overdependence on bookwork with my older kids prepared me for working with him.

If It's Going to Be, It's Up to . . . Who?

"If It's Going to Be, It's Up to Me!"

Have you ever heard that phrase before? It's the kind of "inspirational" saying that Oprah-fied school teachers like to use to encourage their students to do great things. I've even seen posters for the classroom emblazoned with those words. Boy, do I find that phrase annoying! To me, it suggests that anything good or important we might do will develop from our own efforts.

Nothing could be further from the truth. All success comes from God, not from us. We may do things, but if they bear good fruit, that's God's doing, not ours. It's like gardening; we plant the seeds, but God sends the rain and sunshine and makes the seeds sprout.

So what does this have to do with homeschooling? Well, like many people, I began homeschooling with the intention of raising really good kids who would grow into strong, productive, God-fearing adults. That's a worthy goal, of course, but somewhere along the line I began to feel like their development was completely dependent on what my husband and I did while raising and teaching them. Besides being a pretty huge burden to bear, that wasn't true. That kind of thinking was "if it's meant to be, it's up to me" thinking, and it was wrong.

Our children are God's children. True, He gave them to my husband and me to raise, but *with His help*. The success of this child-rearing adventure is totally dependent on God, not on our abilities as parents or mine as their teacher.

But for a while, I forgot that. I researched and bought curriculum as if my children's success or failure in life depended on it. Every time I noticed a flaw in a child's character, I blamed myself and vowed to do something about it. Besides being exhausting (on a bad day, you can find a lot of individual flaws in four kids, and it brings out quite a few of your own, too!), it was sinful for me to believe that raising good kids was all up to me.

God also used other adults in my children's lives to teach them things He wanted them to learn, and that humbled me. I thought that as their parents, my husband and I were responsible for teaching them everything. But God used grandparents, other relatives, neighbors, Sunday school teachers and our pastors to teach them, even if just by example. I came to realize that we would not be the only good examples in their lives unless we moved to a deserted island somewhere.

Once I finally figured out that this child-rearing responsibility was not just up to my husband and me, a burden was lifted. Little decisions like which Bible curriculum to use and whether to let my child play with a certain other child did not have the weight they did before. I prayed about such issues, trusting that God would point us in the right direction, instead of thinking that I had to rely on my own knowledge for everything. That is very freeing!

Now that my children are older, and two are grown, I can see that this was a burden I placed on myself. All through the Bible, we read that all we have to do is ask for help, and it will be given. When it comes to jobs like raising good, God-fearing children, we are not alone. That is an especially important message for fiercely independent homeschooling parents like me. Maybe it's something that you need to hear, too.

As for that slogan I started out with, let's change it to something less burdening and more accurate: "If it's meant to be, it's up to Thee; Please use me." That's an inspirational statement that we can teach our kids without giving them a false sense of power....or burden.

Reclaiming Your Child

An increasing number of the homeschoolers I meet did not "start from scratch" as I did—they pulled their children out of school. There are many reasons why parents do this (a list of them could fill a book), but the common thread is that something was amiss, something serious enough to warrant reclaiming the child and the responsibility for their education.

I admire these parents because they took action. It would be easier to just ignore the warning signs and wait, hoping next year will be better—better teacher, nicer kids, more interesting schoolwork. But love drives these parents to do something about their displeasure with their child's situation.

Pulling a child out of school takes guts, and the longer he was in school, the more challenging it will be to reclaim him. (I'm using the pronoun "he" because probably 90% of the people I've met over the past few years that have pulled their children out of school had sons. I can understand why this happens. Boys are more physically active and even less interested in sitting at a desk all day than girls are. I realize that's a generalization, but the way schools are set up, boys often have a hard time "following the program." Add to that the increasing feminization of schools over time, and you can see why it's not working for a fair number of boys. School personnel often respond to this by suggesting that the most active boys be medicated, yet another big reason why some parents decide to pull their boys out of school.)

Helping your child become the person he was meant to be instead of the person he's been trained to be can be difficult. Marshall McLuhan once said, "The school system, custodian of print culture, has no place for the rugged individual. It is, indeed, the homogenizing hopper into which we toss our integral tots for processing."

When you reclaim your child from the "homogenizing hopper," your instinct may be to provide him with more of the same in an effort to make him comfortable. Re-enacting school at home might feel like the right thing to do at first, but consider that the definition of insanity, according to Benjamin Franklin, is doing the same thing you've always done and expecting different results. Why replicate school at home when school wasn't working for the child? That will not create a new enthusiasm for learning. More likely, it will result in total burnout for your child.

So what do you do with this child whose days are no longer filled with school?

The parents who came before you have found that you must begin deprogramming him. After months or years of being trained in the routines of school, he needs freedom in order to see that there are other ways to live. Neither of you are accustomed to that freedom, so this may not be easy. For you, it probably won't seem like freedom, because you're not used to having him home every day. So this will be a learning experience for you, too. You'll have to be patient; helping him become more self-reliant will take time, but will eventually bear fruit.

The days stretch out before you. If you don't "do school" with him, how will you keep him busy? Busywork is the hallmark of public education, not real education. Your best bet right now is to provide him with learning experiences in an unstructured way, so that he learns to become comfortable with unscheduled time. School trained him to follow its schedule; now you have to train him to follow his own. Instead of diving right into a formal school plan, why not try what has worked for other parents?

You can start by hanging out together at the public library. Encourage him to choose a stack of books to take home. If available, play with educational software together while you're there. Help him get to know the librarians; in time, they will become partners in his learning.

At home, make regular time to read books aloud together and talk about them afterwards. Even older children enjoy being read to; it doesn't seem like work, as independent reading often does. One book I highly recommend is *Diary of an Early American Boy* by Eric Sloane.

The parents I know who have plenty of "deprogramming" experience tell me there are other things you can do before you get to the point of adding any formal homeschooling to your day:

• Visit museums and zoos, letting your child take the lead in deciding which exhibits to look at first. He's used to the teacher calling the shots, but now he needs to learn his own mind.

• Plan meals together. Take him to the grocery store so he can help choose what to buy. Follow recipes together; allow him to do as much of the work as you believe appropriate for his age and skill level.

• Schedule a family vacation (the school year is a great time to do this: lower rates and no crowds!)

• Play age-appropriate board games with your child, including checkers and chess.

• Give your child free reign with art supplies, and the time to be creative.

• Make sure he has ample time to develop and indulge his own interests.

• Put him to work on useful things, like small repairs around the house. This is a good place for dads to get involved, especially if your child has only had female teachers in school.

As he becomes used to the rhythms of home instead of school, you'll want to establish new ways of thinking. Perhaps the most important is the primacy of family over friends. This won't be easy if your child has already become peer-dependent. You'll have to make this change subtly. Don't drop everything for play dates; instead, fit them in around your family's plans. While you don't want to take away your child's social life, the goal is to replace peer dependency with self-reliance as well as increased identification with his own family.

This is also a good time to help your child reconnect with his roots by taking him to visit grandparents and other relatives. Seeing where he comes from will help him reestablish his identity. Spending time with them will help strengthen those family ties.

Encourage individuality and taking the initiative by offering your child choices in clothes, food and daily activities. School, by necessity, encourages conformity and submission to someone else's agenda. By suggesting he choose between alternatives that you have provided, you re-establish your child's autonomy without handing over the reins of daily life to him (you've probably seen the chaos in families where parents have abdicated their roles and put the children in charge.) You also wean him from his dependency on the teacher and school for the patterns of his day.

Take time to listen to him when he wants to talk. What better use of your time can there be than getting closer to your child when he wants to share something with you? As he talks, he will learn more about himself, a sure step on the way to becoming himself again.

All of these things take time, and as the days and weeks go by, you may begin to feel as though you should be "doing school" with him so that he doesn't fall behind. Don't worry; the concept of "falling behind" is a school idea. There are no rules as to when a child should learn something. You want to get back to the idea of self-directed learning, which is the only kind of learning that sticks anyway. If you're worried about his progress, have him tested (privately) in a year or so if it makes you feel better.

It's hard to take the time to deprogram a child who has just come out of a difficult school situation. All that pent-up desire to help him doesn't want to be held back. But it's important to realize that you need to give your child time to find out who he really is, not who he was within the framework of Ms. Smith's classroom, or as a student at Hometown School.

The earlier he began school (or preschool), the longer this could take, so you'll have to be patient. In time, as he becomes reaccustomed to his role in the family and the freedom of being at home, he will become the individual he was meant to be.

When Your Friend Has a Child with Special Needs

I think one of the best things about homeschool support groups is the way one can pull together to support a member who has just had a baby.

Let's face it, we're all very busy, so it's easy to understand just how much it means to the mom with the new baby (whether it's her second or her eighth) to be the recipient of hot meals for a week or two. This form of support is invaluable, isn't it?

Often, one of the expectant mom's friends will begin rallying her homeschooling friends even before the baby arrives. Everyone commits ahead of time to helping the new mom, and they wait expectantly for the news (in our group, it usually arrives by email) that a baby has arrived, and that there's a family that needs congratulations and a hot meal. It becomes quite an exciting time.

But once in a while, the news of a baby's birth comes with something unexpected: the revelation that the baby has special needs. Whether the source of the disability is from premature birth, a birth defect or a birth accident, the lives of an entire group of women are affected by the news. It's hard to know what to do, beyond sending a meal. But this woman and her family will need the support of friends for quite some time, maybe for years, and a meal is just the start. That leaves the question: what else can homeschooling parents do to give support to a fellow homeschooling family with a special needs child?

Having a child with special needs myself, I've got a few ideas for you. I was between support groups at the time Josh was born, but I've been in several groups since then. I also know quite a few homeschooling moms who have children with disabilities, and we've shared our experiences with each other. It's from those discussions that I've come up with some ways you can support a homeschooling family in this challenging situation.

Perhaps you will learn before the child is born that he or she has a birth defect. You can help the baby's mom best by being a good listener when she voices her concerns, and by praying for her, the baby and the rest of the family. When our friends hurt, we want to find a way to solve their problems for them. But this is not a problem anyone can solve. Being there for your friend emotionally is the most you can do besides praying for her.

Once the baby arrives, the way you'd normally respond to the birth of a baby comes into question. Should you send flowers? Do you say congratulations? If you've never been close to someone going through this experience, you may not know what to do.

I cannot speak for all moms, but I can tell you that when Josh was born, I saw a new side to people I thought I knew better. Some people chose to pretend his birth hadn't happened. We heard nothing from them...not a card, not a phone call, nothing. In one case, it was a very close relative who reacted this way, and it was quite painful to me.

On the other hand, I will never forget that the very first thing my brother-in-law said to me after our son's birth was, "Congratulations!" Fourteen years later, how I still appreciate that! And I'm sure he didn't give much thought to saying it. He had grown up with a neighbor family that had a son with Down syndrome, and he thought he was a great guy. So naturally, he congratulated us.

We were also overwhelmed by the outpouring of food from the members of the church we had just joined. We had never met most of these people, but we were lifted up by their prayers, and incredibly grateful for the daily deliveries of home-cooked food that arrived at our home for weeks after Josh's birth. Since we were at the Neonatal ICU every day of that first month, it was comforting to know that our other children and my mother-in-law, who was holding down the fort in our absence, were being well-fed. We also appreciated coming home each night to a meal—what a blessing!

So bring food to the family (some people even brought special treats for our older children), send a card, and if you're not sure what to say, give your friend a hug and let her do the talking. See where she's at emotionally, and take your cue from her.

After some time has passed, new parents of babies with disabilities or medical problems often find that the phone stops ringing, the food donations cease, and they're left to recover alone from the substantial shock of having a baby with special needs. Don't forget your friend! Call regularly, and visit when your friend is ready to have visitors. Once the baby is released from the hospital, ask to hold him. Parents want their new little one to be treated just like any other child.

Often, parents have to take their new baby from doctor to doctor, so that the baby can be assessed and his treatment and therapies can be determined. Offer to babysit the other children in the family; it's so boring for them to be stuck in the waiting room, sometimes for hours, and it can be hard for the parents to concentrate on what the doctor is telling them when their other children are there.

If your friend's husband can't go with to the appointment, another way you can help her (if you can get childcare for your own children) is to go with her so you can serve as moral support. She will also be very blessed if you take notes, so that she has a written record of what the doctor says. Believe me, when your child has a long list of medical problems, taking notes while the doctor talks is very helpful.

As the child grows, his parents will learn different techniques for caring for him, especially if he has medical problems. But those techniques can be time-consuming, and his siblings may feel overlooked. If you can help out by taking some of the children on outings with your own children, you will be doing both the parents and the children a favor.

When Josh was on the apnea monitor for the first two years of his life, our bedtime routine of feeding him (a chore in itself) and getting his leads in the proper position before hooking him back up to the monitor could take as long as two hours. For those two years, we didn't go out much at night, and that limited where our kids could go. Once in a while, someone would offer to take one of them along to a movie or something, and we were very grateful for that!

Taking a Break to Prevent Homeschool Burnout

I hope you've made plans to give yourself a vacation this year, and I don't mean your family vacation to a lake cottage. That's almost as much work as real life! (My mother-in-law says a cottage vacation is just exchanging one kitchen sink for another.)

No, what I'm talking about is a vacation for you—from your chores, your responsibilities, and your routine. We homeschooling moms wear so many different hats. If we don't take the occasional week off, we'll burn out.

Believe it or not, you can do this at home. (Stop laughing and I'll tell you how in a minute.)

First, though, I'll acknowledge that taking a vacation at home is not the ideal situation. When my kids were younger, I used to say I needed to be sent to Mom Camp. That was my wishful thinking vacation spot, where weary moms can spend a few days sleeping, reading novels, eating chocolate, and (when they can summon the energy) sew or make crafts. No cooking, no cleaning . . . just bliss, because all the chores would be done for us at Mom Camp.

While I never found Mom Camp (we probably couldn't have afforded it anyway), I did find that a short vacation at home was just what I needed to rest and regroup. The kids enjoyed the break from our routine as much as I did.

Giving yourself the week off requires you to put things into perspective. The world will not end if you stop cooking and cleaning. Modern civilization as we know it will not screech to a halt because you're taking a breather. Give yourself permission to do this. To ignore your exhaustion is to ask for trouble. Besides, taking a little time off feels so good that once you've done it, you'll wonder why you didn't do it sooner. So why not try it, just for a week?

Here's the plan: get the kids occupied, decide what you want to do with your week, and then give yourself permission to do it. The older your kids are, the easier this will be, but if my email is any indication, the hardest part for us as moms is making ourselves jump off the merry-go-round and take a break from our hectic routines.

Once you've made the decision to do this, what do you do with your children? If they have doting grandparents or other close relatives who would love to take them for a week, that's your ticket. What are you waiting for? You need to do this.

For the rest of us who don't have that option, taking time off is a little trickier, but it can be done. The two main questions we must answer are, 1) how will we keep the kids busy so we can relax, and 2) how will we feed them without having to cook?

First, after doing a major grocery shopping trip (more on that shortly), declare a moratorium on driving for the week you're taking off. Cancel or reschedule everything on the calendar. No classes, no sports, no running around. You're in charge, and you're on hiatus from chauffeur duty. The kids will survive without extracurricular activities for one week. Who knows? You all may decide life is a lot easier when you don't live out of your van. Besides, with gasoline at an all-time high, you'll be saving a nice sum of money by taking a week off from going places every day.

Next, summon your creativity. Keeping the kids busy involves novelty. Bring several new items into the house to keep them busy. Pick up some new toys at garage sales. Get a kiddie pool and a sandbox if you don't already have them; buy a new pool or sand toys if you do. Hang a swing from a tree branch. Make a playhouse (indoor or outdoor) by draping a blanket over a card table or other furniture. Rent some good (and new to your kids) videos or DVDs for them to watch. (Personally, I think it's worth investing in a few things they've been dying to see.)

Most importantly, free them from their usual schedules. Make this week different for everyone. Let them stay in their pajamas all day, as long as they're occupied doing something.

As for the cooking, don't. If you have older kids who want to cook, let them, of course. Otherwise, stock up on yogurt, fresh fruit, and crackers and cheese....easy, simple eats. If you really want to let loose, pick up some of those ridiculously overpriced, microwaveable kids' meals—that's high excitement for the child who's used to home cooking. Pizza rolls, pasta in a can, refrigerated lunch kits....stock up on anything that you don't have to cook. These items probably aren't very nutritious, but it's only for a short time.

While you're at it, make sure you have juice boxes on hand. Little bottles of milk are fun, too. Once again, novelty is important. Whatever you don't normally buy is what you should put on your grocery list. It will cost more than usual, but you'd spend far more if you were actually going on vacation.

While you're at it, let the kids eat on a blanket in the yard, under a tree, or in their treehouse or playhouse, if they have one; in short, anywhere they think it would be fun to eat. Let this week be fun for them as well as for you.

Now that the kids are occupied, what will you do with your time off? That's up to you, but here's what you *won't* do:

- Cooking
- Cleaning
- Opening the mail
- Paying the bills
- Washing dishes (paper plates and cups are the rule this week!)
- Yard work

Resist the temptation. You're trying to get away from your routine, remember? Put those tasks out of your mind. Instead, try remembering who you used to be (before kids) and what you liked to do back then. Did you have a favorite author? If so, plop yourself down with his/her latest novel, and decide that despite any interruptions (there will be, but we hope they'll be few and far between), you're going to keep at that novel until you're finished with it. What will the children think when they see you parked on the sofa with your feet propped up, engrossed in a book? They'll think reading must be fun, because that's all Mommy's been doing lately!

Or, were you an artist or a crafter? Dig out a few of your supplies and play around with them. No pressure, of course...just go back to the days when the things you made weren't eaten, worn or used up within a short time, but actually lasted so you could enjoy them.

There are tons of old television shows on DVD these days. Rent or buy one of your childhood favorites and watch a whole season over the course of a week. You'll feel like a kid again.

Maybe you'd rather spend some time leisurely flipping through magazines, taking up crocheting or writing in a journal. Are you getting the picture yet? The most important thing is to spend some time doing something *you* like to do. It's OK, because you've given yourself permission.

Once you let yourself relax (and you squelch that little voice in your head that says, "But the mail's piling up! And look at the dust on the table!"), you'll start feeling like a new person. You'll be able to tackle those unfinished chores next week, because you'll have more energy. In the meantime, though, you'll be getting a much-needed rest before late summer, when we homeschooling moms tend to kick into high gear. You'll need all the energy you can muster then!

Scheduling Time for Yourself

Vacations (even at-home vacations) are great, but I hope you don't think that one week off a year is enough.

The fact is that being a homeschooling mom is hard work, and you need to give yourself a breather on a regular basis or you'll burn out. While you're busy adding your daughter's soccer games and your son's tuba lessons to your calendar, schedule (in pen!) at least one day a month for you to spend time doing something you like to do.

This is important, but it's not going to be easy. You've got kids, a husband and a home dependent on you. You'll have to make arrangements for that, but it will be so worth it.

Let's look again at your options for making those arrangements for the care of your children. Number one is the Mom Option. If you have a mom, and she lives reasonably close by, ask her to take the kids for a few hours. Maybe you do this already, maybe not. This is your best option, if it's available to you. Go for it!

However, for many of us, the Mom Option doesn't work. You've lost your mom, or she lives far away, or (worst case scenario) she prefers the company of Oprah and Judge Judy to her grandchildren. You need the Husband Option. If you are not already providing your husband and children the chance for quality time together, what are you waiting for? Kids need time alone with their dad, and you need time alone. He needs to work with you on this so you can keep up your energy. Seems like a no-brainer, doesn't it?

But some husbands are always traveling for their work. You may often feel like a single mom. In that case, you need the Friend Option. A like-minded friend is worth her weight in gold.

Recently I spoke with a cool, calm and collected mom who informed me that her children were spending five days with a friend's family. (Now you know why she was so calm!) The two moms had agreed to give each other five days off so they could get their school year planned out, buy books, and spend some time enjoying the peace and quiet. The mom who had the kids took them to the beach, museums and other attractions, while the other mom enjoyed her break. Then the mom with the kids sent both sets to the relaxed mom's house, and she took them places while the first mom got her break. This mom told me they were both very satisfied with how the whole thing worked out.

Whether your help comes from your mom, your husband or your friends, make time for yourself. You'll find yourself much more rested and ready to handle your challenging lifestyle if you do so. In addition, make sure you set aside some time each day for devotions. Get up before the kids, or do your devotions after they've gone to bed. By spending time in the study of God's Word and in prayer, you'll find the strength to get through even the toughest days, and to hang on until you reach your next "day off."

The Freedom You'd Have
If You Sent Your Kids to School

You homeschool your kids? You must be a saint.

Think of the freedom you'd have if you sent your kids to school.

You'd be free to get up at 6 am to drag them out of their warm beds, so they can get ready to go out into the cold to wait for the bus.

You'd be free to mediate the fighting over the bathroom ("No fair! I have to leave first! Make her get out!")

You'd be free . . .

. . . to make sure each one takes the right lunch.

. . . to figure out who left their lunch on the counter.

. . . to send the right permission slips with the right child.

. . . to make sure each one has the right books in the right backpack.

And if there's no bus for your neighborhood, you'd be free to drive the kids to school, along with someone else's kids, if you carpool . . .

Which would leave you free to sit in their driveway honking the horn, shivering and waiting, while your kids fight in the back seat because no one wants to sit next to the kid you're waiting for.

Of course, if you sent your kids to school, now your real freedom would begin, because once the kids are actually in the school building, you'd be free to do what you wanted for an entire six hours:

To clean the whole house all on your own, with no help from the kids.

To watch "Regis and Kelly" or "The View" (didn't you love the time the ladies on "The View" interviewed that famous actor, and to impress them he pulled off their shoes and juggled them? What a great show . . .)

To go shopping, though you can't buy the kids clothes unless they're with, because you don't know what's "in," and they can't wear anything to school that's not "in."

But still, you'd have the freedom to do what you want, uninterrupted . . .

Except, of course, for when the phone rings, and you answer it in case it's the school nurse calling to say one of your kids got sick at school . . . (but of course it's a siding salesperson).

Or when you need to run back to school at 11 am because you're one of the Volunteer Computer Moms (at a school which is already costing you $3,000 a year in property taxes),

Or you're a Field Trip Chaperone, or a Library Mom, or a Room Mom, or an Art Mom, or a Lunchroom Mom.

But still, you'd have freedom for a little while, until it's time to meet the bus or pick up the kids.

Then you'd have to make them all sit down and do homework (even though you feel like a meanie because they just spent all day at school),

And listen to them fight because they're overtired and cranky,

And comfort the one who's crying because "I still don't get what I'm supposed to do!," and you're not much help because you don't see the point of the assignment, either,

And rush them through dinner, because it's almost time to take one to soccer practice, and another to gymnastics, or to Scouts, or to dance class.

And by the time you drop off the last one, the first one will be ready to be picked up, and so you retrace your route, and then head home, where everyone collapses . . .

For a few minutes, but then it's time to make them finish the unfinished homework, and take their baths, and lay out the clothes for tomorrow, and get to bed on time, so they won't give you so much trouble about waking them up at 6 am and dragging them out of their warm beds, so they can get ready to go out into the cold to wait for the bus . . .

Homeschool your kids? You must be a saint.

Think of the freedom you'd have if you sent your kids to school.

ON THE HOME FRONT

Homeschooling is really two full-time jobs: homemaking and educating children. Doing both in the same place makes life even more interesting. Schools may close every night, but the house of the homeschooler is a 24/7 hotbed of activity.

Keeping that house and the people and things inside it organized is the key to successful homeschooling. Hence this final section, which describes how to organize your home and your family, lists tools that will help you in that challenge, shares how we made our house more homeschool-friendly, and provides 115 tips for helping you with all of the above.

Do You Know Where Your Math Manipulatives Are?

Some people make annual resolutions to lose weight or join a fitness center; we homeschoolers resolve to finally locate that terrific science book we bought at the curriculum fair last year, so we can start doing those experiments we promised the kids we'd do together.

I used to put off plans for my children to study a certain subject because I couldn't find the books and resources I needed to use with them. I remembered buying the items; I just couldn't remember what I'd done with them once I brought them home. It was depressing to have to send out a search party every time we needed a specific resource. During our most hectic years, when I was homeschooling and still having babies, I was lucky to find time for even a quick search. My favorite phrase was, "It's around here somewhere!" I needed to get organized.

Who's Got Time to Get Organized?

Homeschooling families buy and use far more books, art supplies and educational toys than other families, but have less free time to organize them. When your children spend their days at home instead of at school, there's rarely a time when they aren't around. Either you get organized with your children underfoot, or it will never get done.

Then there's the thought of how you'd stay organized if you ever got to that point. That's the challenge we homeschoolers face: we live in our houses more than most people, and so do our kids. While other kids are away at school for seven or eight hours a day, ours are at home playing, reading, making art projects, and cooking. The evidence is everywhere. How can we keep on top of all the hustle and bustle?

Lost Opportunities

When you consider trying to get organized with the kids around, it's tempting to stay in your rut and just muddle through, the way you always have. But think about how much time you spend looking for books or resources you need. How many projects do you have on the back burner because you haven't found all the supplies?

In the meantime, your children are growing and changing. If you wait too long to tackle a project, you may find that your child is no longer interested in the subject. A missed opportunity, and all because you couldn't find what was needed, even though you know it is somewhere under your own roof.

Start Out Slowly

The thought of organizing the whole house is way too intimidating to think about. Instead, try starting small. Schedule an hour a day to work on one area that is sorely in need of help. If you're consistent about doing it five days a week, you'll make plenty of progress. Seeing your progress will increase your enthusiasm, and encourage you to keep at it.

Don't decide that your goal is to get the entire house into perfect shape. After all, there are people living in your house every single day. It's not possible to keep it completely organized because it's a continually changing environment. Just work on the areas that bother you most, and have the most effect on your daily life.

For example, while you may long to get your children's baby pictures organized, and maybe even beautifully arranged in a scrapbook, this is not a pressing need. It's more urgent that you find, wash and fold the baby clothes before your new baby arrives.

It may depress you that there are boxes of old tax records scattered around your basement, but it's more important that you find your algebra textbook (and the teacher key!) now that your 12-year-old seems ready to tackle algebra. Try to steer your efforts toward the areas that affect you and your family the most right now.

Establish Systems

As you get an area organized, train yourself, your spouse and your children to keep it that way. Choose specific places to store what you use every day. Make sure everyone knows where things go, and that they will be held accountable for putting the items they use back where they belong. For example, when someone finishes reading a book, it should be put back in the spot where it belongs. Manipulatives should be stored in a designated container in a specific spot; whoever uses them should be held responsible for putting them back properly.

Over time, putting things back where they belong will become an ingrained habit in each member of your family, and your home will stay fairly organized.

Reaping the Results

Be persistent in your organizing efforts. If your family gets hit with the flu and you're forced to give up your daily organizing hour, get back in the groove as soon as everyone is healthy. If the kids won't let you throw out their old toys, send the older ones to watch the younger ones in another room, and then start pitching things quickly and quietly. If you are determined to get the job done, you will.

The resulting small successes will buoy your spirits. Only those who are accustomed to spending days looking for their scissors can understand how good it feels to open the drawer and find them where they belong.

If your enthusiasm for homeschooling has been flagging, this may bring it back. To be able to tackle new projects and finish old ones without wasting a lot of time searching for what you need is a wonderfully invigorating feeling. Don't wait for New Year's Day: resolve right now to experience it.

Top Ten Tools
for Homeschooling Homemakers

Homemaking, when done well, is not an easy job. Family members gobble up all the food you cook, leave footprints on your clean floors, and use up the clean towels and sheets you're forever washing; the youngest (and occasionally the teens) leave nose prints on your just-washed windows. By the very nature of the job, all the work you do soon needs to be done again.

Moms who work outside the home have a hard time juggling homemaking with their jobs, and they get lots of attention and sympathy for this from the media. But at least while they're at work, no one is at home messing up the house or using up all the clean dishes.

We who homeschool have that job in addition to homemaking, and we don't leave home to do it. Our children aren't gone during the day, either. The result is a house that is in use day and night. We will not reach the point where the house stays as we left it until our children have grown and left home.

In the meantime, we need every advantage we can get to help us make a comfortable home while feeding, caring for and educating our families. I've found that one big advantage is having good tools.

The tools on the following list have made my life easier over the past two decades of caring for our family while homeschooling. I learned about most of them as I went along. If even a few of them are helpful to you, then I'm glad. You'll be that much farther ahead than I was when I started out.

First, you really need a **desk**. I used to drool over the big kitchen desks that I saw in model homes—what a great idea! But my kitchen had no room for a desk. Still, the kitchen being the logical place to do my planning, I claimed a section of the countertop and established my "desk." This is where I keep my plan-

147

ning calendar, always laid open and ready for me to write on. In the drawer below, I keep office supplies. In the cupboard above, I store the bills in an upright file, along with restaurant and other coupons.

On the **calendar** on my "desk," I always write down when our library books are due (like most homeschoolers, we go to the public library a lot.) To make sure we don't run up fines, I put a chair near our front door, which is our library chair. That's where I stack the library books when they first come in the house, that's where the kids are supposed to put the books when they are done reading them, and that had better be where I find them on our way out the door for yet another trip to the library. The library chair habit has saved us a lot in overdue fines and lost book charges over the years.

I hate searching through piles of papers for something I really need; after I'd been married a few years, I wised up and made a **home filing system**. This is where I can find income tax papers, the letter from church telling me when I signed up for altar duty, my daughter's orthodontic records and this week's sale flyers for all my favorite stores. You can learn the details of my filing system on page 159.

With four children, two businesses and a homeschool to run, I cannot keep everything in my head. Increasingly, I can't keep anything in my head for long—there are just too many details to keep track of. That's why I have to write everything down. One of the best habits I learned to develop is writing down a **menu plan**. Every weekend, I check to see what food is in the house, and then write down on my calendar what we're having for dinner each day of the coming week. For instance, if I'm making chicken and dumplings on Friday, I write that on Friday's calendar space, and then I write a little note on Wednesday's calendar space reminding me to put the frozen chicken in the fridge to thaw. It is so nice not to think each day about what to make for dinner that night. It's already been decided.

Meals are a huge part of what we do as homemakers; since my family rarely goes out to eat, something is always cooking in my kitchen. This is especially true on the days I use my **crockpot**. By spending a little time in the kitchen early in the day, I get to enjoy the appetizing aroma for hours, and by evening, there's a cooked meal awaiting me. I don't know how people live without crockpots!

Another favorite kitchen tool is my **bread machine**. I use it occasionally to make hot bread to go with dinner, but much more frequently to make dough. Bread dough can be shaped and baked in the oven for a more traditional look, or used to make bread sticks. Pizza dough made with yeast is easy and comes out beautifully. Our favorite is roll dough; I throw a few ingredients in the bread machine after lunch, and by late afternoon I have nice fresh dough to turn into cardamom or cinnamon rolls.

I don't shop at the grocery every day; in fact, I can go well over a week without going there because of my **food stash**. I have shelves and an upright freezer in my basement, so there's lots of room to stash sale items and extra quantities of the items we go through the fastest. You don't have to have a basement to do this. I've heard of homemakers who keep their food stash under the beds, and in a freezer in the garage. Keeping a food stash reduces the number of trips you must make to the grocery, which saves you time and money.

Baking is in my blood (my grandmother worked in a bakery for years). My **restaurant-grade baking sheets** have gotten a ton of use, and yet they are still in good shape. When I bake cookies, I can fit lots of cookies or dinner rolls on each sheet, so I finish up sooner. I line the sheets with foil to bake chicken or fish. I can fit two pies on each sheet; when fruit pies boil over, the sheet catches the mess. I bought my baking sheets at a local restaurant supply store.

The other perpetual chore around here besides cooking is doing laundry. I love anything that makes that chore more pleasant, and I especially love my **clothesline**. I love that it makes our sheets and clothing smell like fresh air while saving me a fortune on utility bills (we have an old clothes dryer). But what I love most about my clothesline is that whenever a washer load is done, I must take a break from correcting algebra or convincing a child that her writing assignment isn't that hard so that I can go outside for a few minutes in the sunshine and hang up the wash. I taught my kids early on that they are not to call for me while I'm hanging clothes unless the house is on fire or someone is bleeding. Those little breaks in the backyard, alone with only the singing birds for company, got me through some very hectic years.

We come now to the most important tool of all. If you've already read my list of "Top Ten Tools for Homeschooling Parents" (page 20), you know that it's **prayer**. When you're a homemaker and a homeschooler, you have two full-time jobs. There's only one place you're going to get the strength for that: ask God. Pray for energy and wisdom and whatever else you need to do your jobs, and you will be given all that and more.

The Homeschooling House

When we bought our house in the late 1980s, we were not yet homeschoolers, but we intended to teach our children at home. It never occurred to us that there might be certain features of a house that would be especially conducive to homeschooling. But over the years, we discovered ways to make our house more homeschool-friendly, and indeed family friendly, and it has made our lives so much easier.

I've been thinking about this lately because we're going to sell our home and downsize. Sarah moved out four years ago, and Peter just graduated from college, got married and moved out of state this year. His room has been emptied of all signs that he lived there except for a few pieces of furniture and a bed.

We still have teenagers Mary and Josh at home, but their needs don't require the kind of space that they did when they were younger and had lots of toys, art supplies and all the other things that younger children like to have access to on a daily basis. They do have computers, books, and other possessions, but our need for space has nevertheless decreased below what it was when we lived here with four active young children.

I keep thinking that it would be nice if a homeschooling family moved in here after us, even though the chances of that are probably pretty slim, statistically. But when I think of all the changes we made here, it seems a shame to waste them on people who are going to park their 1.7 kids in daycare while they go to work each day. This house is meant for a family with kids who have interests, make projects, spend time together, and occasionally need time away from each other.

For instance, there are five bedrooms on our second floor. When we bought the house, it had four bedrooms clustered around a two-story foyer that looked nice, but carried every sound from the first floor to the bedrooms above. It also displayed little ones running around half-dressed in the upper hall to any one who came to the front door. Once we filled the top half of that foyer with the fifth bedroom, our second story became much more private and quiet, and Josh finally had a room of his own, where his nocturnal waking wouldn't bother the others.

Many of today's new homes have two-story foyers, two-story family rooms and even two-story kitchens. Those houses are made for show. Ours is made for a family that lives in it 24/7. Having several two-story rooms also requires a big income (or two) to cover the high utility bills generated by having to heat all that unusable space. But of course, most new houses are not designed for families that use them day and night like homeschooling families do.

Our kitchen was another area of the house that we made family friendly. It started out with a tiny eating area, which was sufficient when we moved here with our 3- and 4-year-old children. However, once we began adding more children, plus needing table space for the many projects and games our children became involved in as they grew up, that little eating area just didn't cut it anymore.

We moved walls to make a huge eat-in kitchen, where the entire family could eat and converse comfortably. We turned the formal dining room into our "schoolroom," where the kids could leave their books out until they came back to them later: no more cleaning off the table to make room for lunch or dinner. It seemed a luxury at the time, but soon became a big timesaver. The extra kitchen space helped me out a lot because I did a lot of cooking for my family of six, plus it left room for someone else to help me while they learned to cook, too.

While we were moving walls, we created an office (with a door, of course!) for my husband, who started an in-home business twelve years ago. For a long time, I joked that I was jealous because I didn't have a door, so I was accessible to the kids all day long. But my husband's door was usually open to the kids, and when it was closed, they knew he could not be interrupted just then. The office was where I sent recalcitrant teenagers who didn't see the point of studying _____ (choose one: algebra, economics, expository writing.)

And then there's our basement. People in our neighborhood tend to finish off their basements so they can have recreation rooms with surround-sound television systems, pool tables, and bars. Not us. Where else do you let the kids finger-paint, play with modeling clay, and roller skate in the winter? We never once had the urge to finish off the only place in the house where the kids could be as messy as they liked!

We have so many fond memories of the years we've spent in this house. But those days are gone, and it's time for us to move on to something smaller and easier to take care of, now that there are only four of us here again. It seems like such a shame to sell this house to people who won't appreciate all the special features of it that make it perfect for a family that actually lives as a family every day. I think we'll just have to pray that it goes to another family of homeschoolers, so that many more years of happy homeschooling can be added to this house's history.

115 Organizing Tips for Homeschoolers

Being a homeschool mom means wearing even more hats than other women: not only are you a wife, a mom, a cook, a laundry service, a cleaning service, and the head purchasing agent, but you are also the teacher. In order to take on all these roles successfully, you've got to get organized.

It's likely that you began homeschooling in a house that was not perfectly organized. Since then, your free time has become rare, and you may believe that you're just too busy to stop what you're doing and put systems into place to make your life and your family's lives run smoother. But when you consider the time wasted by searching for things that you know are "around here somewhere," a little time invested now will save a lot of time later on.

Pace Yourself

A complete overhaul is probably too overwhelming to contemplate, but if you pick an area where you really feel disorganized and tackle it, your enjoyment of the results may lead you to get organized in other areas.

Whether you choose to organize one area of your life or several, don't be discouraged by the amount of time you think it will take. If you work uninterrupted for short, regular periods, you will be thrilled at what you can accomplish. Even an hour a day on the weekdays will lead to amazing results.

Work Solo

That hour, of course, must be spent alone, if you're going to get anywhere. That's why your best chance for success requires that you keep your children out of your way. If you're pitching things, you can't have them there protesting what you've chosen to throw out. If you're going through paperwork, you have to be able to concentrate. You need to find someone to keep the kids busy and supervised for that hour.

If you have babies and preschoolers, your husband, mother or a hired teenage helper (check your homeschool group for candidates) are your best bet. If you have a clingy little one, schedule your hour during naptime. If your husband is the designated child-tender, you may have to work at night.

Reward Willing Helpers

If you have older children, try working for an hour a day while they watch the younger ones. Whether or not you pay the older ones to do this, you'll find that they'll be much more willing to keep the younger ones out of your way if you have offered some kind of reward for their efforts. If actual pay isn't possible, you can pay them with television or video time.

In my household, I paid in Internet time. For every hour Sarah or Peter watched Mary and Josh, they received a credit for 30 minutes of Internet time. Since they both operated their own Web sites, they really appreciated the extra time online.

Stick With Your Systems

After you've organized the areas you need to get a handle on, train yourself to stick with your systems. File, don't pile. Put things away where they belong, and train your spouse and your children to do the same. Once you have a system up and running, it really doesn't take much time to keep it running.

If you get discouraged about getting organized and staying that way, remind yourself of your motivation: to be able to find things quickly, and enjoy whatever it is you're doing because you don't have to keep stopping to look for things.

Emergency Measures

Sometimes, despite your best efforts, an especially busy year leaves you with a house that is so disorganized and such a mess that your head spins just considering where to start. Such a situation calls for emergency measures.

One May I found myself in exactly that situation. Too many activities, combined with homeschooling and some illnesses, left me facing a disaster area.

Since we were taking that summer off of school, I made a plan for resolving the chaos before autumn. I listed all the jobs that needed to be done, from going through everyone's clothes to weed out the outgrown items and those with holes and stains, to washing and ironing the long-neglected window treatments. Then I ranked the chores in order of how much they bothered me, and assigned one per week for the entire summer, starting with the jobs that I felt were the most overdue.

This worked well because I didn't become overwhelmed. Once my weekly chore was finished, I felt great. By the end of the summer, I was mostly caught up around the house, and feeling much better.

Form New Habits

As you work to organize your house for easier homeschooling, look for opportunities to streamline your procedures and your routines. By reading and implementing the following tips, you'll learn which ones save you the most time and effort as you go about your very busy days. Make them habits, and watch your stress level drop as you become more organized.

Homeschooling Tips:

1. Keep a box of homeschool catalogs, making sure to replace old copies with each year's new copies as soon as they arrive. This makes it easier to research something you might need during the school year. You can comparison-shop without having to search all over the house for your catalogs.

2. Don't throw out those old homeschool catalogs just yet. You may want to save them for a friend who is new to homeschooling. After reading them, she can use the contact information to get on all the mailing lists.

3. After a long day of buying out the homeschool convention's vendor hall, or after receiving a mail-order of homeschool books and curriculum, make a list of what you bought and keep it in your homeschool catalog box. This ensures you don't order something you've already bought but haven't used yet.

4. Invest in bookshelves, and arrange all your "school" and children's books by subject or grade level, whichever you prefer.

5. If you have ten spare minutes, ask your children to collect pencils from all over the house, pitch those without erasers, and sharpen the rest.

6. Another way to use ten spare minutes: set the timer and ask your kids to bring every pen and marker they can find before the timer rings. Then set them loose with paper so they can test all of them and throw out the dead ones.

7. Buy a large plastic box (with a lid) for each child's school books and supplies. Let each child decorate their own box with their name and stickers to tell them apart. Keep the school boxes stacked in a corner or cabinet when not in use.

8. Hate to pitch old homeschooling magazines you've already read? Donate them to your homeschool group's library so others may enjoy them.

9. If you use a lesson plan book each year, keep all your old ones together in a place that's easy to access. They're handy to refer to when a homeschooling friend asks you what books you used when your children were studying astronomy two years ago.

10. Store manipulatives in plastic boxes or zippered bags, and keep them, along with small boxes of flash cards and card games, in plastic dishpans. Stack the dishpans, or store them in a cupboard.

11. Store puzzles in zippered plastic bags (inside the original boxes) so you don't lose any pieces. Once a puzzle's box starts falling apart, cut out the actual picture of the puzzle and store it in the bag with the pieces, so you know which puzzle it is.

12. Keep a plastic box of miscellaneous game markers, spinners and dice for board games whose boxes have fallen apart.

13. Get creative with flash cards. Use them competitively with two or more of your children. Toss each card to the first child who answers correctly; whoever ends up with the most cards wins.

14. If you're using flash cards with just one child, let the child keep each card he/she answers correctly, while you keep each card missed. The winner is whoever ends up with the most cards.

15. To paraphrase the old saying, you can't judge educational software by its cover. Before you buy something new, check to see if your public library carries the software you or your children want, and try it at home first.

What to Do With Old Curriculum

16. Old curriculum may not be useful to you anymore, but someone else may really need it. Gather up all the books and resources your family no longer uses, and sell them on the Internet. One good place to do that is www.vegsource.com.

17. Another way to clear out old curriculum is to arrange a swap/sale in your homeschool group. Keep it simple, and plan it for a Saturday so the husbands can watch the kids. Put out the word a month in advance to other homeschool groups, and watch your stuff disappear.

18. Some churches and private schools hold used curriculum sales for homeschoolers. For example, Christian Liberty Academy in suburban Chicago holds a large sale every spring that draws people from miles around. Watch your local newspaper for announcements of such sales, or search for them on the Internet.

19. When you pack away old books and curriculum for the next child, make sure you pack the finished work and workbooks separately from reusable books and supplies. Label such boxes as "Completed School Work" with the child's name. Keep those boxes in the back of your storage area, and leave the front for the boxes containing reusable items, so you can get to them easily.

20. When saving reusable books and curriculum for subsequent children, don't pack them by grade (ex. "Seventh Grade Books"). Instead, box everything by subject. Put all the math books in one box, all the readers in another, etc. This makes it easier to compare the books in a given subject when you are deciding which level to use for your next child.

21. Weed through your educational software. Pitch anything that's scratched or doesn't work anymore. If you have some that work but that your family doesn't need anymore, or doesn't care about, pass them on to friends, or sell them at your homeschool group's next curriculum sale.

Homeschool Files

A filing cabinet is one of the homeschooler's most useful tools. (I don't know how I ever lived without my lateral file cabinet.) You can also use a sturdy cardboard file box instead of a drawer. The important thing is that you have some kind of place to keep files. Manila file folders are inexpensive and work just fine. Here are some file categories for your homeschool file drawer. The suggested file names are in bold print:

22. Make a file for each child's **written assignments**. At the end of the year, pack away the old files and make new ones for the coming year. If your state requires you to keep a portfolio of each child's work, you'll have everything in one place so you can choose the best samples.

23. Make a file for each child's **artwork**. At the end of the year, pack away the old files and make new ones for the coming year. Once again, if your state requires you to keep a portfolio of each child's work, you'll have everything in one place so you can choose the best samples.

24. Make a file for **attendance forms** or any other forms your state may require.

25. Make a file for each child's **achievement test scores and transcripts**. Store photocopies of these reports in the file so you have them available when you need to send them to school authorities or college admissions offices.

26. Make a file for current **community college course catalogs**. You may need a course for your teenager; many community colleges also offer enrichment classes for younger children.

27. If you have teenagers, make a file for **college informa-tion**. Once teens take the ACT or SAT, their contact information is sold; the onslaught of college brochures in the mail begins soon afterward. Keep the brochures on file until your teen makes a college decision.

28. If you have a teenager nearing college-age who intends to go to college, make a **FAFSA** file. The FAFSA is a form you must file with the U.S. government each year to determine if your teen is eligible for financial aid. Since the FAFSA comes from a government agency, you can expect lots of paperwork to arrive in the mail, and all of it must be kept on hand.

29. Make a **memento** file for each child. This is where you file the ticket stubs from the play your child performed in, the programs from concerts your child performed in, and award certificates and ribbons. It's also a good place to put photographs of your child participating in extracurricular activities.

30. Make a file for all invoices and shipping tickets from **homeschool catalog mail orders**.

31. Make a file for your **homeschool group**'s newsletters, directory, notes from meetings, and other paperwork.

32. Make a file for **field trip** possibilities, including ads and articles about different sites, museums and factories you've read about.

33. Clip and keep a file of **articles about homeschooling**. You never know when you might want to show some to a skeptical relative, or a friend who needs encouragement. Store photocopies of your favorite articles in this file so you can hand them out without losing your originals.

34. Keep a file of **teacher keys** for the books you're using this year that don't have answer keys bound into the student copy.

35. If you use a **correspondence curriculum**, make three files: one for **billing**, one for **report cards**, and one for **general information** about the curriculum. Should you stop using the correspondence curriculum, be sure to transfer the report cards to each child's "Achievement Test Scores and Transcripts" file (see tip #25).

Personal Records and Files

As a homeschooler, you're running a large operation, and you need a "command center" to help you stay on top of things. Dedicate a specific area for your command center. It could be as simple as a section of countertop in the corner of your kitchen, or as elaborate as a built-in desk area located in a convenient part of your house. Here you can keep your personal calendar, office supplies, and everything else you need to keep your home and family running smoothly.

36. If you don't have a desk, try using a plastic dishpan to store stationery, pens, and other supplies. Slide the dishpan into one of your upper cabinets to store it out of sight. When you sit down to pay bills, etc., take the dishpan with you.

37. A three-ring binder comes in handy for keeping records that you add to on a daily basis. It doesn't have to be anything fancy. Just make a divider and sheet for each section, and keep the binder in an accessible spot, preferably near your kitchen or command center. Mine includes sections for:
- daily expenses
- monthly financial profile
- date of magazine arrivals
- Christmas card registry
- a list of which gifts we've bought for family and friends
- a list of rebates I've sent out
- a list of birthdays and anniversaries

38. I make the above lists on sheets of notebook paper, but if you want something already made up for you, visit some of the wonderful organizational sites on the Internet for free household forms. Entering the phrase "home organization" in a search engine will get you started.

39. Keep a large opaque plastic box filled with medical supplies up high in your kitchen, either on the top shelf of a cabinet, or in the soffit area, if you have one. We call ours the Sick Box, and it contains a thermometer, various medicines and fever reducers, bandages, and ointments.

40. Keep a spiral notebook near your Sick Box. We call ours the Sick Book. When one of our children becomes ill, we start a new page in the book, noting the date, time, body temperature and symptoms of the child, along with when and how much medicine or fever reducer we gave them, changes in body temperature, and other pertinent details. Checking the Sick Book prevents you from giving doses of medicine too close together, and provides you with information for when you call or visit the doctor's office.

41. If you're bleary-eyed from being up several nights in a row with sick kids, take your Sick Book (see previous tip) with you. Hand the book to the doctor and let it do the talking for you.

Here are some file categories for your personal file drawer. The suggested file names are in bold print:

42. Make a file for each child's **medical and dental records**. Once in a while, ask the pediatrician's office staff to photocopy your children's vaccination record chart. Put the date on it, and keep it in this file.

43. Make a file for grocery and other **sale flyers**. Replace the old flyers as you receive new ones.

44. Make a file for each child's special papers related to **activities**, so you won't have to search the house for one child's scout campout permission slip or another's gymnastics medical form.

45. Make a file for this year's **taxes**. This is where you can file anything you may need for tax reporting, including receipts for charitable donations, property taxes and medical/dental fees.

46. Make a file for **receipts**. Use it to store receipts for expensive items, especially furniture and appliances, as well as clothing. Some stores will allow the return of a defective item, or one that didn't last very long, even a year or more later if you have the original receipt.

47. Make a file for **take-out menus and fast-food coupons** if your family orders out often.

Calendars

If you really want to stay on top of things, you need two calendars. The first, a **destination-only** calendar, is described in the next tip, and is meant for the use of the entire family. The second, your **personal** calendar, is meant only for your use, and should include notations of anything and everything that you must remember. The more you write down, the less you have to keep in your head. So write it down!

48. Keep a **destination-only** calendar on your refrigerator or in another prominent spot. On it list only events, appointments and work hours: no birthdays, reminders or anything else. A quick glance will tell you who needs to go where that day without wading through notations of whose anniversary it is or that it's time to flip the mattresses.

49. Train your teens to write their work hours on the destination-only calendar as soon as they receive their schedules.

50. To keep a calendar on the fridge, attach a long piece of magnet strip, available at craft stores, to the back of the calendar across the top.

51. In your **personal** calendar, jot down the next time you need to do a household task; for example, after you clean the refrigerator, write "clean refrigerator" for the day six months from now. This allows you to put it out of your mind until then.

52. Write on your personal calendar the due dates of library books and rented videos and DVDs.

Coping with Mail and Bills

53. Staying on top of the mail is one of the best habits you can cultivate. Make a habit of sorting through it every day. Weed out the garbage and recyclables first, and the rest won't seem so overwhelming.

54. Next, pull out all bills and other date-sensitive materials. Write down each bill and its amount on your personal calendar, seven days before the due date. Now you know how many dollars' worth of bills must be sent out each week without digging through the actual bills.

55. Keep your bills together in a specific spot, so you can find them easily. If you're limited on desk space, or don't want your bills out where they can be seen, buy a small plastic vertical file that you can keep in a cupboard, and reserve one slot for bills. Other slots can be used for restaurant coupons, scissors, tape, or keys.

56. Pick a day each week to write out all the bills for the coming week, or pay them online.

Keeping Track of Phone Numbers

57. The inside of each of your upper kitchen cabinet doors is prime information space. Tape business cards inside one, making sure to include those of your family's doctors, dentists and other medical professionals.

58. Inside another upper cabinet door, tape a customized phone list that includes not only the phone numbers of your family, friends and neighbors, but also other numbers you call frequently, including the local library, pool, grocery store, other retail stores, and your favorite pizza place. You may have these programmed into your phone already, but a babysitter or other visitor to your home might not know how to access them.

59. Another useful phone list consists of the names and numbers of everyone you deal with in your homeschool group and/or co-op, as well as those you may need to call because of your children's activities, including troop leaders, music instructors, coaches, and playgroup members.

Saving Time and Money

60. When you make medical or dental appointments, ask for the first appointment after lunch. Most of the time, you won't have to spend very long in the waiting room.

61. Keep all receipts for a few weeks so you'll know where to find them when you need to return or exchange something. If you don't have space for a vertical file, keep them in a large manila envelope in a drawer or cupboard. When the file or envelope is full, go through and pitch those you're certain you won't need, and file the rest (see Tip #46).

62. Save the return envelopes that come with junk mail, and use them to make your shopping lists. Coupons can be stored inside, so you don't have to search for them once you reach the checkout.

63. Always shop with a list. A little time spent at home making lists from the sale flyers you keep in your file cabinet (see Tip #43) will save a lot of time later in the store.

64. Prevent last-minute shopping runs for one item you need right that minute. Train yourself, your spouse and your children that when there is only one left of something, put it on the shopping list. Keep your list on the refrigerator, where everyone can find it.

65. Never go out for just one thing if you can help it. For example, if you need to stop by the post office, check your shopping list for anything you need that can be bought at stores in the vicinity of the post office. Combining stops saves time and gasoline.

Get Yourself Organized

66. Buy a handbag that works *for* you, not against you. Make sure it has enough room for everything you need when you're away from home for a few hours or for the day. Some have a cell phone pocket, which makes it easy to find your phone quickly when it's ringing.

67. If you have babies and/or toddlers, try trading your handbag for a fanny-pack or a back-pack. They keep your hands free for holding on to little ones.

68. Decorate a sturdy cardboard box, or buy a plastic box with a lid, and write "Mom's: Keep Out!" on it. Inside, store your postage stamps, stationery, envelopes, pens, thank-you notes, and a nice selection of sympathy and get-well cards. When you work on correspondence, you won't have to waste time searching for the things that often walk away.

69. Keep note pads and pencils on your night table, in your bathroom, in the areas you work with your children, in the kitchen, and in your vehicle. When your child is reading aloud and you suddenly remember something you need to add to your calendar, you can write it on the pad, then forget about it and go back to paying attention to the child. When you're in the shower (where busy moms often do their best thinking) and you remember that you're supposed to call someone back, you can make a note to yourself once you get out. And when your child says or does something funny, you can write it down and toss the paper in their Baby Box (see Tip #77).

70. Check your local school district's Web site to find out which days are designated as teacher institute days, conference days, state and federal holidays, and half-days. Those are bad days to run errands; with all the kids off of school, the stores are crowded, and there's lots of screaming and tantrums (and that's just the moms). Instead, use those days to stay home and enjoy family time.

Running Your Home

A smoothly running home is everyone's goal, but it requires a lot of work and organization to achieve. A family is a constantly changing organism, and since homeschooled children are home during the day, the house and its contents are always in use. Everything you cook and clean will soon be used up or made dirty, and will have to be done again. Establishing and following routines for keeping up will prevent you from becoming overwhelmed. Here are a few ideas:

71. If you have a multi-level home, consider buying duplicates and triplicates of items you use all the time, including scissors, tape, thermometers, vacuum cleaners and cleaning supplies. Put one on each level of your home.

72. You won't run out of clean clothes, linens or towels if you schedule weekly laundry days. After a while, it becomes a habit to do each on a certain day, so you never find yourself without clean things.

73. If you feel overwhelmed by all that must be done around the house, establish specific days of the week for certain chores beyond the laundry. You won't waste time feeling guilty that the carpets need to be vacuumed if you know tomorrow is vacuuming day.

74. In order to train your children to pick up after themselves, establish a Confiscation Box. When our children were younger, I confiscated anything they left out overnight. My intention was to hide the item for a few days, but often I forgot where I hid it, so it might be quite a while before they saw it again. That certainly taught them not to leave things around! A box will allow you to confiscate items without losing them. Just make sure you keep it up high, where it can't be rescued easily.

75. Once only available in mail order catalogs, over-the-door hooks and racks can now be bought in most discount and dollar stores. Use a pair to hide your ironing board behind your bedroom door, or to hang extra towels in a bathroom. If you're using a closet-less room for a child's bedroom, a few over-the-door hooks allow dress clothes to be hung up on hangers.

76. Buy some inexpensive timers, and keep one near the computer and another near the television. Use them to set limits on usage, and also to time each user when there are several children taking turns using the computer or choosing television shows or videos. You can even use one for yourself, so you can limit your time online if you need to do so (time flies when you're online, doesn't it?)

77. Are some (or all) of your children lacking a lovingly filled-out "baby book"? Buy each child a plastic box with a lid, and call it their Baby Box. Get into the habit of tossing little notes about what the child said and did into it, along with the outgrown teddy bear or blanket you just can't part with, the first pair of shoes, the list of measurements from each doctor visit, etc. Don't stop as they grow older, either. Some of the things they say as adolescents will amuse you (maybe not right now, but eventually!) Someday you may find time to assemble baby books, but even if you don't, each child's treasures and memories will be in one place if you've gotten into the Baby Box habit.

78. Do your children have too many clothes? Most children wear their favorites, leaving many nice things unworn until they're outgrown. Homeschooled kids don't need as many different outfits and shoes as kids who go to school. If you weed out what your children don't wear, and only buy what's absolutely necessary, you'll find more room in the closets and more money in your wallet.

79. Give each of your children a 4-inch square of light-colored construction paper or cardboard to put their name on and decorate. Laminate these, and keep them on the kitchen counter. Now when they use a cup to get a drink, they can park the cup on their square and use it again, instead of taking a clean cup each time. If you don't have access to a laminator, use clear contact paper on both sides.

80. Keep all of your household's appliance manuals in plastic pockets in a binder. You'll always be able to find a manual when you need it.

81. Buy a high-quality map (or map book, if you live in or near a city) and keep it in a designated, easy-to-access place near the door. Then you can grab it on your way out to garage sales, field trips, or anywhere else in an area that's not familiar to you. Make a habit of replacing it in the same spot when you get home.

82. Keep antibacterial gel in each car's glove box; require each child to use some after outings and especially before eating in the car. You'll be surprised at how well it keeps them from getting sick.

83. If you frequently record shows and movies off the television, or make many home movies, you are probably overrun with homemade videocassettes or DVDs. Number all of them, and ask an older child to stack them in numerical order in your video cabinet, while making a master list of what's on each tape or DVD. Now you can check your master list instead of trying to read the side of every tape or DVD in the cabinet when you're looking for a certain show or event that you recorded. One of your children can be assigned the job of keeping them in numerical order.

84. Feeling desperate, like you'll never catch up? Try changing your weekly schedule to four days of school, and use Friday as your "catch up" day. It's amazing how much you can accomplish on that one day. To work out a yearly schedule this way, take the number of school days per year your state requires, divide by four, and plan that many four-day weeks of school each year.

Stashes

Companies need warehouses; households need stashes. A stash is an area set aside for the storage of things your family often needs, so that you'll have them on hand the instant you need them. It's hard for moms, especially those with small children, to run out every time something is needed. Living that way is inefficient for everyone.

Keeping stashes of necessities allows you to be prepared for whatever happens. Keeping track of what's in your stash allows you to replenish your supplies on a regular basis, and also saves you money, because you'll have time to wait for things to go on sale instead of being forced to pay the going rate because you need it immediately. Here are some ideas for stashes for your household:

85. Always keep a stash of cough drops, acetaminophen, aspirin, bottled water and soft drinks. Should both parents get sick at once, there will be supplies in the house, and no feverish parent will have to drag themselves to the store.

86. Set aside an area away from the kitchen for a stash of canned goods, dry goods and detergents. Stock up when such items are on sale and store them there. Be sure to rotate your stock (use the oldest first).

87. Set aside an area in your basement, garage, closet or even under a bed for a stash of toilet paper, facial tissue and paper towels.

88. Keep a stash of birthday, anniversary, baby, sympathy and get-well cards so you don't have to run out to the store at the last minute before a party, or when you hear of an event or a need.

89. Keep a school supply stash, and replenish it every July, when school supplies go on sale. Some items, like glue sticks and notebook paper, are 75% cheaper during the "back-to-school" sales than they are the rest of the year. Don't buy more glue sticks than you can use in a year, though; they dry up if you keep them too long.

90. Using one or more large plastic covered boxes, keep a stash of craft supplies, including markers, rubber stamps, blow pens, stickers, craft sticks, felt, trims and anything else your children might use to create something.

91. Keep your own private stash of markers, pens, tape and a stapler. Do not let your children even know it exists. This will save your sanity more than once.

The Public Library

Homeschoolers tend to spend a lot of time in public libraries, and they bring many books and resources home. Keeping track of them will prevent you from running up big fines.

92. When you bring home library books, immediately write the due date(s) on your personal calendar.

93. Another way to keep track of library books: before you leave the library, take a stack of books and photocopy them from the spine sides, so you end up with a picture of all the books you checked out with their titles and call numbers.

94. Library books and materials should be kept in a specific place, such as on a foyer bench or in a plastic container, in the room where your kids do their schoolwork, so they don't disappear. Train your children to return all library materials to that spot when they're finished with them.

95. If your children bring library materials along in the car for entertainment, keep a basket or tote bag in the car, and train the children to put the materials into it when they're finished.

96. One of the biggest time-savers around is your public library's Web site. You can use it to look for books, request them, and have them held for you. You can check your account to see if you have any overdue books (homeschoolers often do!), and if so, what fines are owed. You can renew books with a few clicks. And you can do all of these things in your pajamas at midnight!

Living (and Homeschooling) with Small Children

It's hard to keep some semblance of order in your home when you have small children. It's even harder to work with older children while your younger ones are around, but you must. One way to keep things on an even keel is to control the environment, with a goal of keeping the little ones occupied and content. This means regular meals, regular naps, and a toddler-proofed house. Here are a few tips that will help:

97. Use your younger children's schedules to determine the best times for doing certain things. For example, it's a lot easier to explain algebra to your 13-year-old while your toddler is napping, than when he's wide awake and making demands. On the other hand, recitations and other oral activities can be done when the younger children are around; they may even learn from them.

98. Tape yourself reading aloud your preschooler's favorite book, and say "Turn the page now!" at the appropriate places. Listening to this book-on-tape will keep your child busy when you need to work with another child.

99. Keep a box of special toys for your toddlers and pre-schoolers that can only be played with when you are working with your older children. The novelty of these toys will buy you some time for teaching while the little ones are on the loose.

100. Use educational software with your preschoolers. They pick it up quickly, learn a lot from it, and it buys you some time with your older children. As with the toys mentioned in the last tip, if you reserve the software for only those times when you're working with your older children, it will seem more special to your preschoolers.

101. They aren't as popular as they used to be, but for short periods, nothing beats a play pen. Set it up by your school table, and train your baby or toddler to spend a short while there each day. They can play happily with you in sight, while you work with the older children.

102. Don't let children under age ten have access to all of their toys. Keep half in reserve (packed away in boxes somewhere). On days when you have a lot to do, exchange them for the toys your children have been playing with most recently. It's like Christmas all over again, as your children rediscover toys they forgot they had. While they're busy playing with their "new" toys, you can get something done without interruption . . . or just take a breather.

103. Set aside a corner for an "office" for your preschoolers and younger children to keep them busy while you work with the older children. Search garage sales and rummage sales for an old adding machine or an old typewriter, as well as file trays. Fill the trays with junk mail letters, forms and especially envelopes. Add a few pencils, and let the kids loose. You'll be amazed at how much they enjoy working in their "real" office.

104. If you have a very active baby or toddler, one who doesn't let your family get much done school-wise, consider taking some time off of studies completely, and change your focus to outings and field trips for a while. Active children often do better with a frequent change of scenery. Put the little one in a back-pack, front-pack or stroller, and make daily excursions to parks, nature museums, zoos and anywhere else your children like to go. Your older children will still be learning, and you'll appreciate the change, too.

105. Many homeschoolers spend a lot of time in the car. If you have a child who tends toward car sickness, keep a coffee can with the lid attached to the bottom in each of your vehicles.

Should someone get very carsick, they can throw up in the coffee can, and you can put the lid on and pitch it afterwards.

106. Keep a spare set of clothes in your car for each pre-schooler. If you store the set in a plastic bag, you can put soiled clothes in the bag for the trip home.

107. Put hook-and-eye locks at the top of the bathroom and bedroom doors to keep out little marauders while you're busy with homeschooling or other things. If any of your little ones like to go outside without permission, consider putting hook-and-eye locks at the top of all your exterior doors to prevent escapees.

Keeping Up Your Energy

As a homeschooling mom, you have a challenging job, and you need to take good care of yourself in order to handle it. Here are a few tips to help you:

108. Rest time is golden. Establish an hour in the after-noons when everyone goes to their own room or bed and rests. Younger children can nap, older children can read or draw, and Mom can do whatever she needs to do (go for the nap; you won't regret it). The earlier you start this habit with your children, the easier it will be to get them trained.

109. Make an effort to buy something small here and there to pamper yourself. Whether it's a bar of imported soap, a few of your favorite chocolates, or a new pair of earrings, use small treats to keep up your spirits.

110. When it seems like you and your children have been out running to activities too much, take a day off. Don't go any-where; just hang out at home playing board games, making popcorn and watching old movies. Give yourself permission to do this. The entire family will thank you.

111. Find a park with a jogging path around it, or a gym with a track around it (try your local YMCA), and arrange for some homeschool gym days. While the kids play in the middle of the park or gym, the moms (with little ones in strollers or backpacks) can do laps and talk. You'll all go home refreshed.

112. Take occasional breaks in your school day. When you sense that your child's attention span has reached its limit, stop for a snack or a stretch. There's nothing noble about working for several hours straight.

113. As with any job, accept that you will have some bad days. When you need a shoulder to cry on, take a break and call your husband or a good homeschooling friend, and vent for a few minutes.

114. If your homeschool group doesn't offer a monthly Mom's Night Out, get one started. Meet at a coffee shop or other public spot where food is available. Don't plan an agenda; just relax and enjoy getting to know other moms who know just what your life is like.

115. Count your blessings. Try to enjoy every stage of each child's development. Most of all, realize that someday they will be grown and gone, and you will have ten times as many memories as other moms, because you were there with them every day.

INDEX

What is *Life Prep for Homeschooled Teenagers*?

It's a curriculum that teaches teenagers skills and values they'll need in the adult world they're about to enter.

It walks them through processes like....

♦ researching a place to live
♦ figuring out health insurance
♦ understanding credit
♦ learning about basic investing

.... with an attitude of prudence, and a goal of minimizing debt.

It also reviews concepts they'll need for....

♦ getting along with family, friends, coworkers and clients
♦ finding a spouse
♦ living their values, and making sure those values are reflected in their work

.... and helps them reflect on the principles you've taught them since they were small.

Literature and mathematics are important, but so is getting ready to take on the adult world. Barbara Frank designed this curriculum for her own teenagers so they would have some preparation for living on their own. They worked hard and learned a lot, and are now independent young adults. She hopes that *Life Prep for Homeschooled Teenagers* helps you prepare your own homeschooled teenager for life "out of the nest."

Praise for
Life Prep for Homeschooled Teenagers

Reviews from the First Edition of *Life Prep for Homeschooled Teenagers*

"Both because of the content and the design, I think homeschoolers are likely to find this one of the most practical and important resources for high school."

Cathy Duffy, author of
100 Top Picks for Homeschool Curriculum

"I highly recommend this book for anyone with older children. While I am doing this with my daughter now at age 16, it would certainly be a beneficial study for 14- and 15- year-olds as well. Actually, I'm hoping *I* might learn something."

Terri Miller, Staff Writer • *The Old Schoolhouse Magazine*

"*Life Prep for Homeschooled Teenagers* is an amazing resource designed for those preparing to leave home."

The Virginia Home Educator

"I can tell you that by using this book as it is intended you will save your children much future grief.... Barbara Frank has put together a clear, helpful guide that covers more than I had thought of myself, in putting together a list of what our teen needs to know before she sprouts feathers and flies the nest."

Eclectic Homeschool Online • www.eho.org

"High school students will likely find these projects meaningful and relevant, as they teach something students this age are eager to learn: what you need to know to live on your own.
P.S. - Many young (and not-so-young) adults may find this resource useful, too!"

Cindy Prechtel's Homeschooling From The Heart
www.homeschoolingfromtheheart.com

Cardamom
Publishers

Visit www.CardamomPublishers.com

LaVergne, TN USA
18 October 2009

161251LV00004B/91/P